Wired into Teaching Torah

An Internet Companion

Scott Mandel

A.R.E. Publishin RMC
Denver, Color 222
MAN

Published by:
A.R.E. Publishing, Inc.
Denver, Colorado

Library of Congress Control Number 2001088668
ISBN 0-86705-049-7

Printed in the United States of America
10   9   8   7   6   5   4   3   2   1

Dedication

This book is dedicated to my great-grandparents, Alter and Fanny Jaffe; my grandmother Anna Mendelowitz [z"l]; and my grandmother in Cleveland, Rose Hinds. These significant individuals helped shape my love for Judaism and enabled me to share our heritage with my own children.

Acknowledgements

I want to give special thanks to my editors, Rabbi Raymond A. Zwerin, Audrey Friedman Marcus, and Steve Brodsky of A.R.E. Publishing, Inc. Their expertise and guidance were invaluable in bringing this book to fruition.

I am also indebted to Melodie Bitter, Ben Zion Kogen, and Robert Schuck, who reviewed the manuscript, tried out the web sites, and offered their excellent ideas, suggestions, and insights.

Finally, my sincere thanks go to all of the educators and programmers who took the time to place on the Internet their educational accomplishments. Through their commitment and energy, they have made the cyberworld an online Jewish educational utopia.

CONTENTS

INTRODUCTION

Mrs. Meyer was teaching Genesis to her sixth grade students. In particular, she was covering the Torah portion *Lech Lecha*, and was discussing the verses in which Abram becomes involved in a war with his neighbors. As a curricular resource, she was incorporating activities suggested in the book *Teaching Torah*[1]. In Activity #6 under the section marked "Strategies: Extending the Text," she came across an interesting modern day concept concerning how nations should treat each other in times of war. This was material that paralleled the *parashah* verses that her class was reading, and was extremely relevant to their discussion:

> The Geneva Convention established a code of behavior for nations at war. Read through the section relating to soldiers, behavior regarding prisoners and spoils of war. Compare this to the behavior of the warring nations in this portion . . . . (p. 22)

Mrs. Meyer thought that this was an excellent learning opportunity for her students, especially since they were covering related material in their secular studies. However, she did not have a copy of the Geneva Convention accessible. Her synagogue library did not have one, nor did her public library. Although she eventually found an address to which she could write and request a copy, she decided that, after spending more than three hours on this search, it was not worthwhile to continue. She chose to abandon this particular idea and simply go on to the next Torah portion.

[1] Sorel Goldberg Loeb and Barbara Binder Kadden. *Teaching Torah: A Treasury of Insights and Activities* (Denver, CO: A.R.E. Publishing, Inc., 1997).

Unfortunately, this is too often the scenario for many excellent curricular ideas. Teachers in both small and large schools, in both rural and urban communities, often have difficulty locating supplemental curricular resources. Either the cost to acquire the materials is prohibitive, or the search for them takes significantly more time than the lesson is worth. Luckily for Mrs. Meyer, in today's technologically advanced society, there exists an educational resource that allows teachers in any size school, in any size community, quick and easy access to a wealth of supplemental curricular material. This innovation is the Internet — "The Ultimate Teacher Resource Center."

Let us alter the last paragraph of the above anecdote so that it reflects teaching in the twenty-first century, incorporating the limitless resources of the Internet:

Mrs. Meyer thought that this was an excellent learning opportunity for her students, especially since they were covering related material in their secular studies. However, she did not have a copy of the Geneva Convention accessible. Her synagogue library did not have one, nor did her public library. Knowing the vast amount of material available on the Internet, Mrs. Meyer went online and typed in this URL: www.unhchr.ch/html/menu3/b/91.htm (see Figure 1).

Within seconds, she had displayed on her computer screen the complete text of the Geneva Convention. Mrs. Meyer printed a copy and brought it into her class, providing her students with an interesting and worthwhile extension of the biblical text they were studying.

The Purpose of This Book

This book is designed to provide immediate Internet resources for many of the various activities suggested in the A.R.E. publication *Teaching Torah*. When incorporating one of the strategies in that book into your lesson, you can simply go to the URL listed on these pages and find a wealth of supplementary resources — maps, drawings, photographs, and detailed explanations of obscure or archaic terms. All that is required is a computer at home — school or student online access is not a prerequisite. It should also be noted that the material

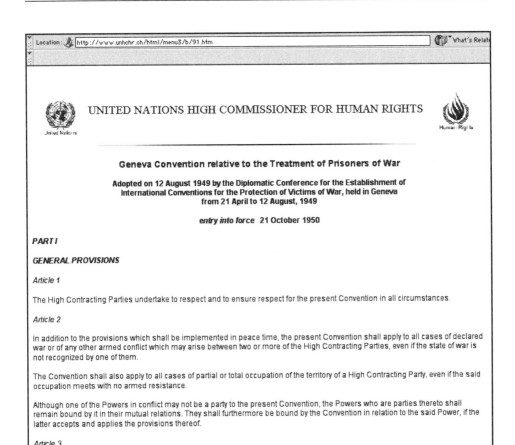

FIGURE 1: A portion of the screen showing the Geneva Convention relative to the Treatment of Prisoners of War.

included in this work extends beyond *Teaching Torah*, and can be used with any curriculum concerned with the teaching of the Torah.

The process is both simple and extremely worthwhile. Curricular ideas that might not be attempted in class due to a lack of materials can now be easily integrated into your teaching on a regular basis. Following are some quick examples of how using the Internet resources listed in this book can immediately enrich your teaching, regardless of the Bible curriculum you are using.

You want to show your students the various journeys of the patriarchs, and to identify locations throughout Canaan in which they lived. A MAP OF ANCIENT ISRAEL can be found at: www.wsu.edu/~dee/HEBREWS/ANISRMAP.HTM (see Figure 2).

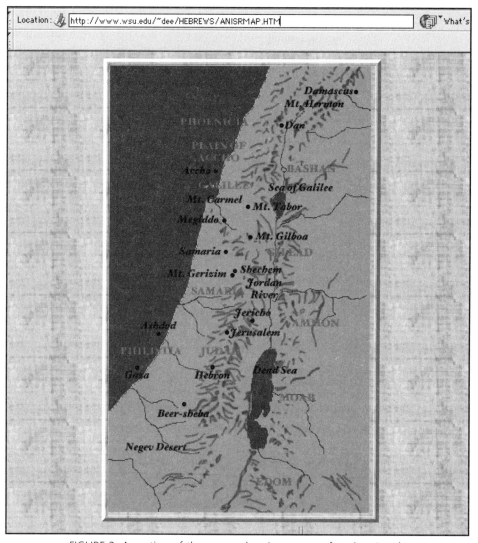

FIGURE 2: A portion of the screen showing a map of ancient Israel.

During a discussion of the story of Noah and the Flood, questions were raised about extinct and endangered species. Material on ANIMALS: LIVING, EXTINCT AND ENDANGERED can be found at: www.worldwildlife.org (see Figure 3).

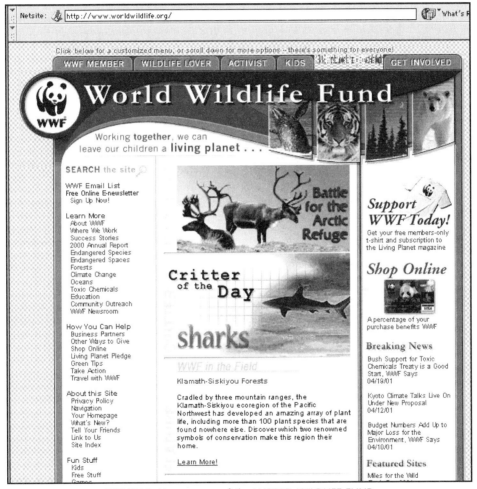

FIGURE 3: Home page of the WORLD WILDLIFE FUND.

Just before beginning to teach the book of Exodus, you wish to find background material on the Egyptian culture to which the Israelites were exposed and in which Moses was raised. You can find a wealth of

information on the CULTURE OF ANCIENT EGYPT at: emuseum.
mankato.msus.edu/prehistory/egypt/history/history.html (see Figure 4).

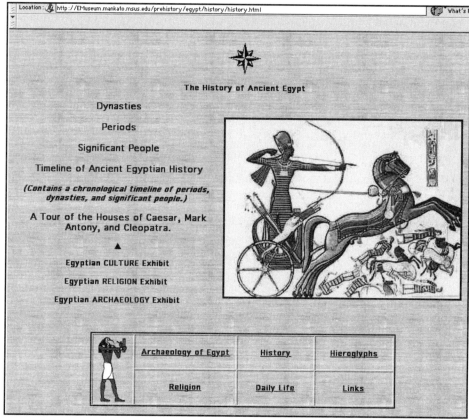

FIGURE 4: A portion of the screen showing material on Egyptian culture and history.

Your students learn that the Israelites ate quail while they traveled
through the desert. However, most of these students have never seen a
quail. You can find a PICTURE OF A QUAIL at: www.ngpc.state.ne.us/
wildlife/quail.html (see Figure 5).

Your students are discussing some of the laws of *kashrut* as presented in the Torah. As they review the material, they have a number of
questions concerning *kashrut* in today's society. A treasury of information on KASHRUT can be located at: www.kashrut.com (see Figure 6).

FIGURE 5: A portion of the screen describing quail.

These are just a few examples of the ways in which you can immediately enhance your Torah curriculum through the use of supplemental resources found on the Internet.

How to Use This Book

The material in this book is meant to supplement your existing Bible curricula. This book does not provide teaching strategies or suggestions on how to teach the Torah to your students; the *Teaching Torah* book noted above (and/or your school curriculum) provides various teaching ideas and directions for your classroom activities. Rather, this

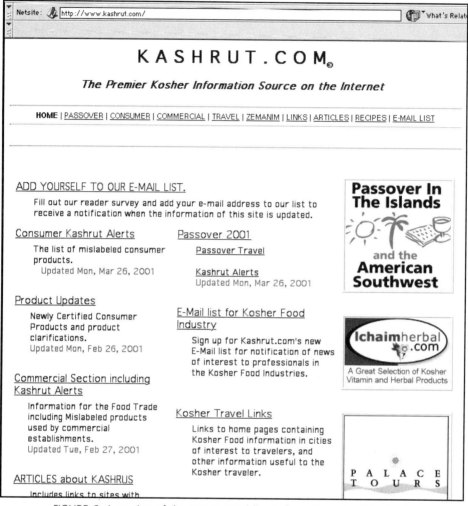

FIGURE 6: A portion of the screen providing information about *kashrut.*

book gives you Internet resources to enhance and extend those teaching strategies you might select in order to fulfill the goals of your particular Torah curriculum.

Wired into Teaching Torah is divided into three sections: Internet Resources by Torah Portion, Internet Resources by Topic, and Commentator Resources.

Internet Resources by Torah Portion

This section directly parallels *Teaching Torah*, portion by portion. For example, you would use one of the Internet sites presented in this resource if:

- *Teaching Torah* mentions a particular term, item, or concept that you would like your students to explore in greater depth.
- *Teaching Torah* suggests a teaching strategy that could be enhanced by material found on the Internet.
- *Teaching Torah* mentions an organization to contact for more information on a particular topic. If that organization has a web site, the URL will be listed here.

As you work through *Teaching Torah*, simply refer to this section each time you begin a new portion.

Please note that although this book contains well over 300 listings, not every term, item, or concept mentioned in *Teaching Torah* can be found on the Internet; nor does every organization mentioned there have a web site. However, the world of cyberspace is constantly evolving, and by the time you read this book a link may well have been established. Therefore, if there is something in *Teaching Torah* that is not listed in this book, refer to "What to Do If Something Can't Be Found Online" (page xix) for tips on how to discover quickly if a new online resource exists.

Internet Resources by Topic

This section is most valuable for those who are not using *Teaching Torah*, but are incorporating a different curriculum as they cover the Torah in their classroom. As you come to a new topic of interest, refer to this section to see what Internet resources are available.

Although most items in this section are arranged alphabetically, a number of subject areas have been grouped together. These are topic areas such as animals, archaeology, art, Judaism (denominations of), holidays, maps, organizations, and vegetation.

A number of sites contain material that will be useful for several different Torah portions, and you may wish to "bookmark" these sites so that you can return to them easily in the future. For instructions on bookmarking, see Appendix B on page 129.

Commentator Resources

This section provides background material on various Torah commentators mentioned in *Teaching Torah*. Information on the lives and work of most of the major commentators can be found through these URLs. Know that the majority of material available on commentators comes in the form of a reference in someone else's commentary, rather than as specific biographical information. Generally, this section does not include modern day, living commentators, whose work is current and readily available commercially.

How to Use Material Found Online

Once you have found supplementary material online using the URLs listed in any of the above three sections, you can:

▪ Print out the pages that you want to use in their entirety[2]. Bring to class one copy as a teacher resource, or make duplicates for your students.

▪ Select certain portions of the material, such as a map or picture, which you wish to use. Copy and paste the section into a blank page in your word processing program, and then print out that page. This choice also allows you to add descriptions or titles if you choose. Bring in one copy as a teacher resource, or make duplicates for your students.

▪ Bookmark the site so that you can return to it easily in the future. For instructions on bookmarking, see Appendix B on page 129.

---

[2] Please note the copyright laws in your state. Most states have what is referred to as a "Fair Use" policy. This policy allows teachers to print material found on the Internet for classroom distribution only, as is described in this book.

What to Do If Something Can't Be Found Online

The Internet is rapidly evolving, and millions of new pages are added every week. Internet sites come and go quickly, usually without advance notice. Therefore, some of the sites listed in this book may not exist when you attempt to access them, or may be temporarily unavailable. If that occurs, do not panic; rather, go through the following simple steps:

1. Check carefully the text you typed to make sure that it matches EXACTLY the address given in this book. If one letter is incorrect or a "dot" or "/" is in the wrong place, your browser will be unable to find the requested page. Also note that URLs are case sensitive, meaning that typing the proper capital and lower case letters is critical. Active links to all the sites listed in this book can be found on the A.R.E. Publishing, Inc. web site at www.arepublish.com/wired.html.

2. Wait a day or two. Internet sites "go down" for a variety of reasons, including:
   - Weather conditions that affect telephone data lines. For example, a storm in Atlanta can affect Internet access in Los Angeles. Internet data travels all over the world via routes that are hard to fathom.
   - Site maintenance may be in progress, which can cause a site to go off-line for a few days while being updated or for equipment upgrades.
   - Jewish religious observance. A number of Orthodox sites shut down on Shabbat and Jewish holidays.

3. Attempt to access other pages of the site, working upward through the hierarchy until you reach the root page. For example, when searching for A MAP OF ANCIENT ISRAEL you typed in www.wsu.edu/~dee/HEBREWS/ANISRMAP.HTM, but perhaps found that page unavailable. Try retyping the address, leaving off the text at the far right of the address, including the last slash: www.wsu.edu/~dee/HEBREWS — then push "enter" or "return." In this case the

server tells you that you are not authorized to view this page. Try again, moving up one more level: www.wsu.edu/~dee. Now you are able to view a page, hosted by Washington State University, that contains material on World Civilizations. By exploring the links on this page, you may be able to find the map you originally sought. Finally, you can move up one more level and access the "root" page of the site at www.wsu.edu, which takes you to the home page of Washington State University in Pullman, Washington. This trick can also be useful in determining something about the organization that hosts a particular page or site. The great thing about the Internet is that in the course of browsing and exploring various links you just might find something even more valuable or interesting than the original document you were seeking.

4. Do a meta-search of the topic, the name of the item, person, or organization. Use a meta-search engine such as METACRAWLER (www.metacrawler.com) to ascertain if the URL has been changed, or if an alternate site now exists. Simply type in the name of the item, person, or organization that you wish to find in the search box, select the "phrase" button (if the search term contains more than one word), and press "search" or hit the "return" button on your keyboard. You will be provided with a list of links and descriptions, which you can use to see if a site provides material which suits your needs.

5. Do a full search using general search sites, secular educational and Jewish educational sites. This is a more lengthy, although valuable, process, and well beyond the scope of this book. Detailed information on how to conduct a full Internet search for curricular materials can be found in *Wired into Judaism: The Internet and Jewish Education* by Scott Mandel (Denver: A.R.E. Publishing, Inc., 2000). That book provides you with a step-by-step description of how you can locate easily and systematically virtually any curricular resource on the Internet. The book also contains two very important sections that are both valuable and relevant to any search for Internet materials that you may undertake:

- A section entitled "How to Evaluate Internet Sites" provides a form you can use to evaluate the worth of sites, taking into account their pedagogical outlook (i.e., Orthodox/Reform, Israeli right wing/left wing, Jewish/Christian/secular), and the educational value of the material that the site contains. It should be noted that several of the sites referenced in this book are sponsored by Christian organizations, and contain Christian content and references, interspersed with information that is both valuable and pertinent to the study of Torah. This section of *Wired into Judaism* will help you sift through this type of material.
- A section entitled "Accessing Hebrew Web Pages" walks you through the steps to configure your computer properly so that you can display pages that are written in Hebrew.

Additional Tips

Here are a number of potential areas of concern that you may have as you go through the Internet sites listed in this book:

Commercial Sites: Some of the listed sites are commercial in nature, in particular those which contain ritual objects. However, these sites often provide photographs or drawings that can be valuable in the classroom. To copy a picture, right-click on the image, select "copy," then paste the image into a new word processing page. Add any captions or descriptive text and print. Of course, you can always simply print the entire page directly from the site and bring it to your students.

Non-Jewish Sites: Some of the best material on the study of biblical issues can be located at non-Jewish sites. Since you are searching for teacher resources versus student-read material, this should not present a significant problem. Simply edit the material as needed. For a detailed explanation of the importance and benefit of using non-Jewish sites in your Internet searches, along with a form on how to evaluate these sites, see *Wired into Judaism*.

Organizational/Judaism Sites: The URLs to these sites typically direct you to the organization's main (or "home") page. You may have to explore the site a bit to locate the exact material that you require. If you are unable to find the material you desire, an e-mail address will often be posted, allowing you to contact the organization with any questions you may still have.

Small Pictures/Graphics: Most of the pictures of objects and art are rather small on the screen. These are called "thumbnail" graphics. Often, when you move your cursor over the picture it will turn into a hand with a finger pointing. This means that you can click on the picture to see an enlarged view. You can then print the enlarged picture for your students, or copy and paste it into a new word processing document.

Part 1:
Internet Resources by Portion

The following section parallels the suggested activities and teaching strategies listed in *Teaching Torah* for each portion. If you are using that resource, visit the following URLs to find supplemental material that will enhance your students' study of any particular *parashah*.

If you are not using *Teaching Torah*, but rather are incorporating your own school's Torah curriculum, then use the material listed in each of the portions below as a supplemental guideline for covering the biblical material presented to your students.

The sites listed below are just a starting place — there is much more material available in cyberspace than could possibly be listed here. As you browse the Internet, don't be afraid to follow the links you find — they'll take you to many additional interesting and valuable sites.

Updated active links to all the sites listed in this section can be found on the A.R.E. Publishing, Inc. web site at: www.arepublish.com/wired.html.

GENESIS

BERESHEET
Genesis 1:1-6:8

Animals: Living, Extinct and Endangered
www.worldwildlife.org
www.defenders.org
www.bagheera.com

Enuma Elish (Babylonian Text)
web2.airmail.net/capella/aguide/genenum.htm

Lilith
www.lilitu.com/lilith/historical.html

Maps: Ancient Middle East
www.khouse.org/blueletter/images/maps/Otest/world.jpg

Organizations: American Society for the Protection of Nature in Israel (see Figure 1-1, page 4)
just-tzedakah.org/reports/SocietyfortheProtection/
basicinfo.html
www.spni.org/e/

FIGURE 1-1: Home page of THE SOCIETY FOR THE PROTECTION OF NATURE IN ISRAEL.

Organizations: Friends of the Earth
www.foe.org

Organizations: Sierra Club
www.sierraclub.org

Organizations: World Wildlife Fund
www.worldwildlife.org

Planets
pds.jpl.nasa.gov/planets

Vegetation: General
endeavor.des.ucdavis.edu/cnps/thums.asp

NOAH
Genesis 6:9-11:32

Animals: Living, Extinct and Endangered
www.worldwildlife.org
www.defenders.org
www.bagheera.com

Archaeology: Ur (see Figure 1-2, page 6)
EMuseum.mankato.msus.edu/archaeology/sites/
middle_east/ur.html

Biographies: Modern Individuals
amillionlives.com

Boats: Ancient
www.arksearch.com
www.lexiline.com/lexiline/lexi143.htm

Gilgamesh (Babylonian Text)
pubpages.unh.edu/~cbsiren/assyrbabyl-faq.html#Gilgamesh

Maps: Ancient Middle East
www.khouse.org/blueletter/images/maps/Otest/world.jpg

FIGURE 1-2: This page about the ancient city of Ur typifies the wealth of information that can be found at the EMuseum web site.

Olympic Rings

www.southcom.com.au/~jennifert/Games/rings.html

Organizations: Jewish Vegetarian and Ecological Society

www.ivu.org/jvs

Organizations: Jewish Vegetarians of North America

www.orbyss.com/jvna.htm

Organizations: Local Tzedakah Opportunities
www.volunteermatch.org

Organizations: Vegetarian Resource Group
www.vrg.org

Rainbows
www.unidata.ucar.edu/staff/blynds/rnbw.html
australiansevereweather.simplenet.com/photography/
photos/1994/0626mb01.jpg

Vegetation: Olive Trees
www.gilboa.co.il/ol-tree.htm

LECH LECHA
Genesis 12:1-17:27

Archaeology: Ur
EMuseum.mankato.msus.edu/archaeology/sites/
middle_east/ur.html

Brit Milah/Circumcision
www.mishpacha.org/britabout.shtml

Desert life: Travel (see Figure 1-3, page 8)
www.interknowledge.com/egypt/sinai/bedouin.htm

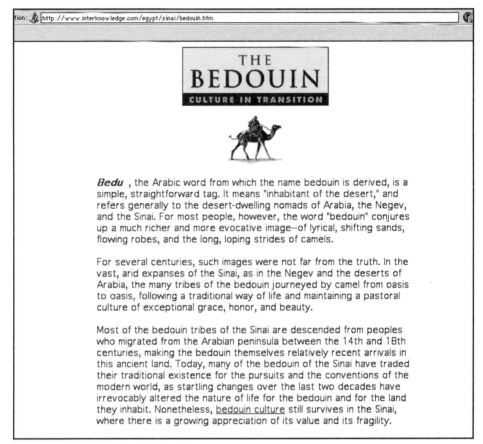

FIGURE 1-3: From this page about the Bedouin tribes of the Sinai,
you can find additional information about Bedouin culture.

Geneva Convention
www.unhchr.ch/html/menu3/b/91.htm

Maps: Ancient Israel
www.wsu.edu/~dee/HEBREWS/ANISRMAP.HTM

Maps: Ancient Middle East
www.khouse.org/blueletter/images/maps/Otest/world.jpg

Names
www.behindthename.com

VAYERA
Genesis 18:1-22:24

Animals: Rams (see Figure 1-4, page 10)
raysweb.net/wildlife/pages/02.html

Desert Life: Tents
www.interknowledge.com/egypt/sinai/bedouin02.htm

Jerusalem: Church of the Holy Sepulchre
www.us-israel.org/jsource/Archaeology/church.html

Jerusalem: Dome of the Rock
www.us-israel.org/jsource/Society_&_Culture/geo/
Mount.html#Dome

Jerusalem: Via Dolorosa
www.us-israel.org/jsource/vie/Jerusalem2.html#Cross

Maps: Ancient Israel
www.wsu.edu/~dee/HEBREWS/ANISRMAP.HTM

Shofar
www.holidays.net/highholydays/shofar.htm
www.judaicaonline.com/CT_Misc/PRMS2_MSG427.htm

Location: http://raysweb.net/wildlife/pages/02.html

▶ next
◀ back
◀ links to this animal
◀ thumbnail index
◀ email
◀ home
◀ photo links
◀ gallery sales

Photo Credit: Jamie Ruggles

Big Horn Sheep

The Big Horn Sheep [Ovis canadensis] is a large North American species with a brown coat, which turns to bluish-grey in winter. It is so named from the size of the horns of the ram, which often measure over 1 m/3.3 ft round the curve.

FIGURE 1-4: Here is an image of a bighorn sheep, which is similar to a ram.

CHAYAY SARAH
Genesis 23:1-25:18

Chevrah Kaddisha
www.shemayisrael.co.il/burial/index.htm
www.jrf.org/cjcmd/chevrapg.htm

Desert Life: Wells
www.hia.net/kjsmith/imagint/algeria.htm

Maps: Ancient Israel
www.wsu.edu/~dee/HEBREWS/ANISRMAP.HTM

Organizations: MAZON
www.mazon.org

Organizations: Rabbanit Bracha Kapach
www.ziv.org/z2k_023.html

Vegetation: Tamarisk Trees (see Figure 1-5, page 12)
www.members.tripod.com/~bbowles/tamarisk.html

Weddings
www.ohr.org.il/judaism/articles/wedding.htm

TOLEDOT
Genesis 25:19-28:9

Desert Life: Wells
www.hia.net/kjsmith/imagint/algeria.htm

Firstborn Rights
www.newadvent.org/cathen/06081a.htm

Maps: Ancient Israel
www.wsu.edu/~dee/HEBREWS/ANISRMAP.HTM

Location: http://www.members.tripod.com/~bbowles/tamarisk.html   What

The Tamarisk Tree

This Tamarisk Tree Photo is Copyrighted by:
James L. Reveal, Norton-Brown Herbarium, University of Maryland.

FIGURE 1-5: This web site (see URL location at the top of the screen), which shows a tamarisk tree, is well known for its photography.

Organizations: Jewish National Fund (see Figure 1-6, page 13)
www.jnf.org

VAYAYTZAY
Genesis 28:10-32:3

Archaeology: Ancient Idols (see Figure 1-7, page 14)
www.eliki.com/ancient/civilizations/sumerian

FIGURE 1-6: Home page of the JEWISH NATIONAL FUND.

Archaeology: Bethel
www.execulink.com/~wblank/bethel.htm

Maps: Ancient Israel
www.wsu.edu/~dee/HEBREWS/ANISRMAP.HTM

Twelve Tribes
www.hadassah.org.il/chagall.htm

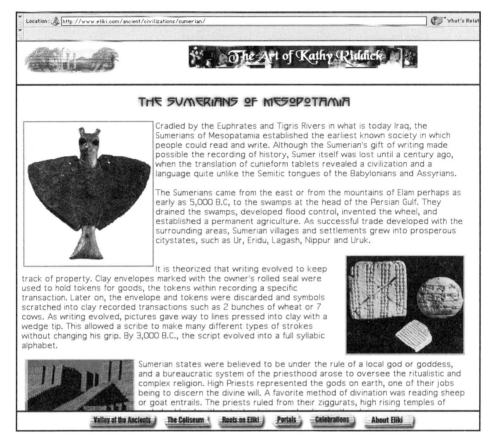

FIGURE 1-7: This web page provides information about ancient Sumeria, as well as pictures of Sumerian idols and other items of cultural importance.

Weddings

www.ohr.org.il/judaism/articles/wedding.htm

VAYISHLACH
Genesis 32:4-36:43

Amalek

aish.com/holidays/purim/haman_heir_to_amalek.asp

Archaeology: Ancient Idols

www.eliki.com/ancient/civilizations/sumerian

Archaeology: Cairo Genizah

www.lib.cam.ac.uk/Taylor-Schechter/Introduction.html

Archaeology: Shechem (see Figure 1-8, below)

www.maxpages.com/shechem

Brit Milah/Circumcision

www.mishpacha.org/britabout.shtml

Genizah

www.brittanica.com/seo/g/genizah

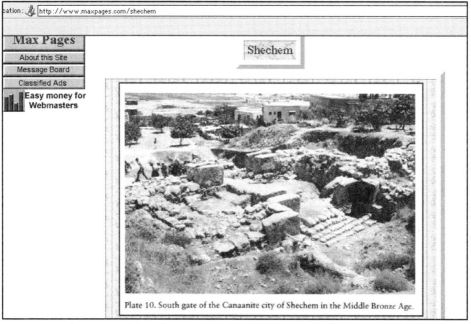

FIGURE 1-8: This web page provides archaeological information about the Canaanite city of Shechem.

Kashrut

www.kashrut.com

www.kosherfinder.com

Maps: Ancient Israel

www.wsu.edu/~dee/HEBREWS/ANISRMAP.HTM

Names

www.behindthename.com

VAYAYSHEV
Genesis 37:1-40:23

Egypt: Ancient Culture

emuseum.mankato.msus.edu/prehistory/egypt/history/
history.html

Joseph's Coat

www.reallyuseful.com/joseph

Maps: Ancient Egypt

www.khouse.org/blueletter/images/maps/Otest/world.jpg

Organizations: American Red Cross (see Figure 1-9, opposite)

www.redcross.org

Organizations: American Red Magen David for Israel

www.armdi.org/main.html

FIGURE 1-9: Home page of the AMERICAN RED CROSS.

MIKAYTZ
Genesis 41:1-44:17

Egypt: Ancient Culture
emuseum.mankato.msus.edu/prehistory/egypt/history/
history.html

Maps: Ancient Egypt (see Figure 1-10, opposite)
www.khouse.org/blueletter/images/maps/Otest/world.jpg

Organizations: American Jewish World Service
www.ajws.org

Organizations: Amnesty International USA
www.amnesty-usa.org

Organizations: MAZON
www.mazon.org

Organizations: Oxfam America
www.oxfamamerica.org

VAYIGASH
Genesis 44:18-47:27

Egypt: Ancient Culture
emuseum.mankato.msus.edu/prehistory/egypt/history/
history.html

Maps: Ancient Egypt
www.khouse.org/blueletter/images/maps/Otest/world.jpg

Maps: Ancient Israel
www.wsu.edu/~dee/HEBREWS/ANISRMAP.HTM

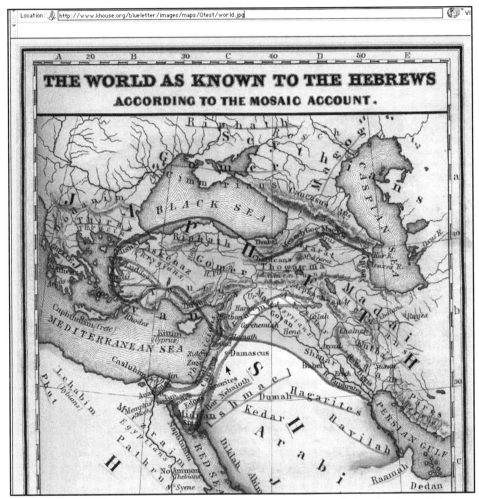

FIGURE 1-10: A portion of a map showing the world as known during the time of Moses.

Organizations: American Jewish World Service
(see Figure 1-11, page 20)

www.ajws.org

Pope John XXIII

www.newadvent.org/Popes/ppjo23.htm

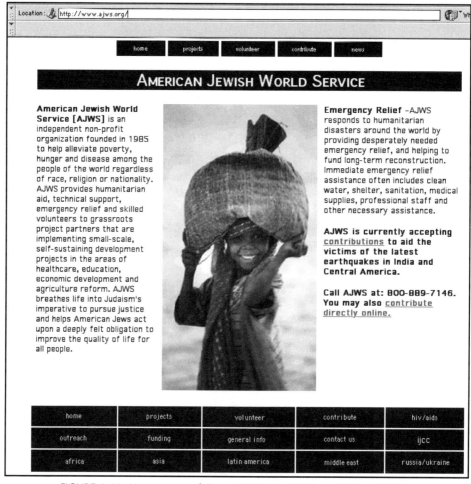

FIGURE 1-11: Home page of the AMERICAN JEWISH WORLD SERVICE.

VAYECHI
Genesis 47:28-50:26

Egypt: Ancient Culture
emuseum.mankato.msus.edu/prehistory/egypt/history/
history.html

Ethical Wills
www.ethicalwill.com

Maps: Ancient Egypt
www.khouse.org/blueletter/images/maps/Otest/world.jpg

Maps: Twelve Tribes
www.khouse.org/blueletter/images/maps/Otest/boundaries.gif

Twelve Tribes (see Figure 1-12, page 22)
www.hadassah.org.il/chagall.htm

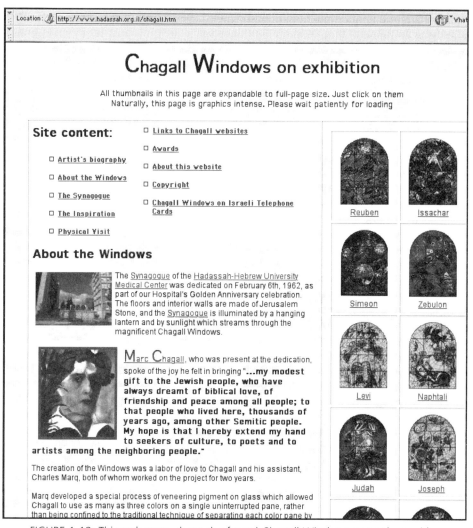

FIGURE 1-12: This web page about the famed Chagall Windows not only provides general information about the Twelve Tribes of Israel, but also background about Marc Chagall, the creator of the windows.

EXODUS

SHEMOT

Exodus 1:1-6:1

Brit Milah/Circumcision
www.mishpacha.org/britabout.shtml

Egypt: Ancient Culture
emuseum.mankato.msus.edu/prehistory/egypt/history/
    history.html

Maps: Ancient Egypt
www.khouse.org/blueletter/images/maps/Otest/world.jpg

Organizations: Bay Area Council for Jewish Rescue and Renewal
www.bacjrr.org

Organizations: World Union Task Force on Soviet Jewry (UCSJ link)
www.fsumonitor.com

Twelve Tribes
www.hadassah.org.il/chagall.htm

VAERA
Exodus 6:2-9:35

Egypt: Ancient Culture
emuseum.mankato.msus.edu/prehistory/egypt/history/
history.html

Maps: Ancient Egypt
www.khouse.org/blueletter/images/maps/Otest/world.jpg

Organizations: Local Tzedakah Opportunities
www.volunteermatch.org

The Ten Plagues (see Figure 2-1, opposite)
www.shul.org.za/pesach/plagues.html

BO
Exodus 10:1-13:16

Animals: Lambs
www.mindspring.com/~zoonet/pinemoun/pictures/sheep.jpg

Animals: Locusts
www.earthlife.net/insects/images/orthopta/locusta.jpg
www.ris.net/~lawnman/bible.html

Egypt: Ancient Culture
emuseum.mankato.msus.edu/prehistory/egypt/history/
history.html

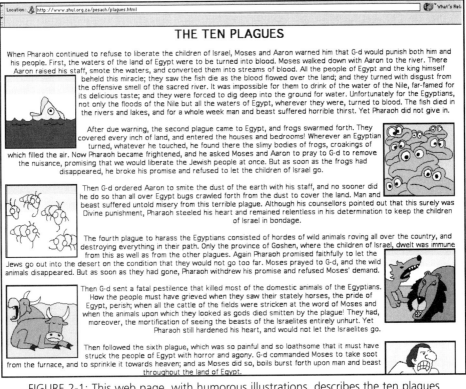

FIGURE 2-1: This web page, with humorous illustrations, describes the ten plagues that were visited upon Egypt before Pharaoh let the Hebrews go.

Firstborn Rights

www.newadvent.org/cathen/06081a.htm

Holidays: Passover

207.168.91.4/vjholidays/pesach/Home.htm

www.holidays.net/passover

Maps: Ancient Egypt

www.khouse.org/blueletter/images/maps/Otest/world.jpg

Matzah
aish.com/holidays/passover/articles/immediate_changes.asp
graphicdesign.miningco.com/arts/graphicdesign/library/
    passover/blpasclip1.htm

Pidyon HaBen (see Figure 2-2, opposite)
www.us-israel.org/jsource/Judaism/Pidyon_Haben.html

Tefillin
www.tefillin.co.il
www.mjoe.org/ritual/tefillin1.html

The Ten Plagues
www.shul.org.za/pesach/plagues.html

BESHALACH
Exodus 13:17-17:16

Amalek (see Figure 2-3, page 28)
aish.com/holidays/purim/haman_heir_to_amalek.asp

Animals: Quail
www.ngpc.state.ne.us/wildlife/quail.html

Challah
www.bus.ualberta.ca/yreshef/shabbat/shabcustoms.html
biblicalholidays.com/Sabbath/challah.htm

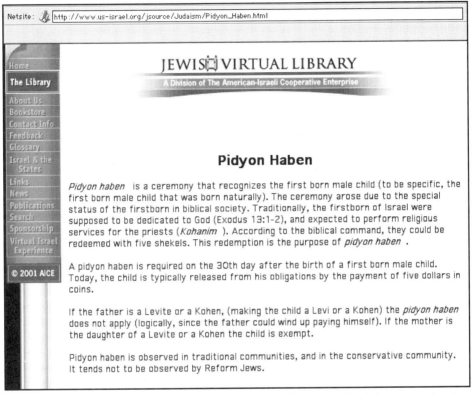

Netsite: http://www.us-israel.org/jsource/Judaism/Pidyon_Haben.html

JEWISH VIRTUAL LIBRARY

A Division of The American-Israeli Cooperative Enterprise

Home
The Library
About Us
Bookstore
Contact Info
Feedback
Glossary
Israel & the States
Links
News
Publications
Search
Sponsorship
Virtual Israel Experience

© 2001 AICE

Pidyon Haben

Pidyon haben is a ceremony that recognizes the first born male child (to be specific, the first born male child that was born naturally). The ceremony arose due to the special status of the firstborn in biblical society. Traditionally, the firstborn of Israel were supposed to be dedicated to God (Exodus 13:1-2), and expected to perform religious services for the priests (*Kohanim*). According to the biblical command, they could be redeemed with five shekels. This redemption is the purpose of *pidyon haben*.

A pidyon haben is required on the 30th day after the birth of a first born male child. Today, the child is typically released from his obligations by the payment of five dollars in coins.

If the father is a Levite or a Kohen, (making the child a Levi or a Kohen) the *pidyon haben* does not apply (logically, since the father could wind up paying himself). If the mother is the daughter of a Levite or a Kohen the child is exempt.

Pidyon haben is observed in traditional communities, and in the conservative community. It tends not to be observed by Reform Jews.

FIGURE 2-2: This web page, from the Jewish Virtual Library, contains information about Pidyon Haben, the ceremony that redeems the firstborn male child.

Egypt: Ancient Culture

emuseum.mankato.msus.edu/prehistory/egypt/history/
history.html

Maps: Sinai

www.khouse.org/blueletter/images/maps/Otest/sinai.gif

FIGURE 2-3: In addition to the subject of Amalek, this web page contains a wealth of information and activities related to Purim.

YITRO
Exodus 18:1-20:23

Holidays: Shabbat
www.shabat.co.il
www.jewfaq.org/shabbat.htm
www.everythingjewish.com/Shabbat/Shabbat_Origins.htm
www.ou.org/chagim/shabbat

Holidays: Shavuot (see Figure 2-4, below)
207.168.91.4/vjholidays/shavuot
www.holidays.net/shavuot

FIGURE 2-4: The Shavuot page from the VIRTUAL JERUSALEM web site. Note that the URL of this site begins with a series of numbers instead of the more familiar www.

Judaism: Conservative
www.uscj.org

Judaism: Orthodox
www.ou.org

Judaism: Reconstructionist
www.jrf.org

Judaism: Reform
www.rj.org
www.uahc.org

Ketubah
www.theketubah.com

Laws of Other Cultures: Code of Hammurabi
www.wsu.edu/~dee/MESO/CODE.HTM

Maps: Sinai
www.khouse.org/blueletter/images/maps/Otest/sinai.gif

Organizations: Local Tzedakah Opportunities
www.volunteermatch.org

Shofar
www.holidays.net/highholydays/shofar.htm
www.judaicaonline.com/CT_Misc/PRMS2_MSG427.htm

U.S. Judicial System
encarta.msn.com/find/Concise.asp?ti=06747000
www.firstgov.gov/us_gov/judicial_branch.html

MISHPATIM
Exodus 21:1-24:18

Animals: Oxen (see Figure 2-5, below)
members.aol.com/zoonet/pictures/gaur.jpg

FIGURE 2-5: The ZOONET web site is an excellent resource for photos of animals, such as the Gaur, a type of ox, pictured here.

Holidays: Passover
207.168.91.4/vjholidays/pesach/Home.htm
www.holidays.net/passover

Holidays: Shabbat
www.shabat.co.il
www.jewfaq.org/shabbat.htm
www.everythingjewish.com/Shabbat/Shabbat_Origins.htm
www.ou.org/chagim/shabbat

Holidays: Shavuot
207.168.91.4/vjholidays/shavuot
www.holidays.net/shavuot

Holidays: Sukkot
207.168.91.4/vjholidays/sukkot
www.holidays.net/sukkot

Kashrut
www.kashrut.com
www.kosherfinder.com

Laws of Other Cultures: Code of Hammurabi
www.wsu.edu/~dee/MESO/CODE.HTM

TERUMAH
Exodus 25:1-27:19

Animals: Calves
www.kidsfarm.com/red.htm

Menorah (see Figure 2-6, opposite)
www.templeinstitute.org/vessels/menorah.html

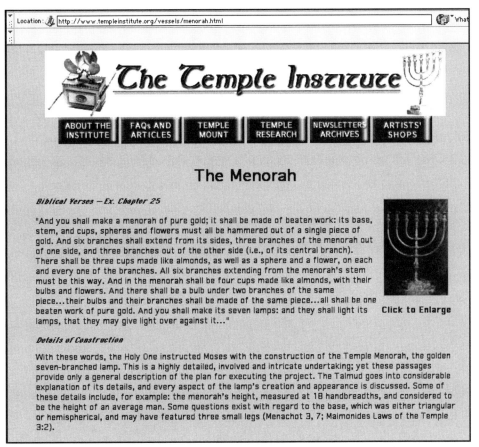

FIGURE 2-6: This page from the TEMPLE INSTITUTE web site includes a description and construction details of the *menorah*.

State of Israel – Symbol

www.knesset.gov.il/knesset/tour/etour2.htm

Synagogues

www.mlandau-architects.com/synagogue.htm

The Tabernacle

www.domini.org/tabern/tabhome.htm

TETZAVEH
Exodus 27:20-30:10

Archaeology: Lamps (see Figure 2-7, below)
members.tripod.com/~Oil_Lamps

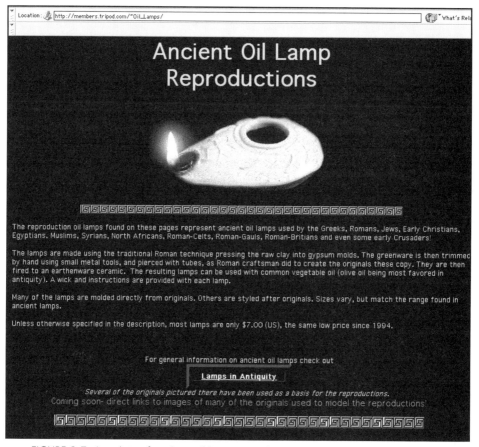

Location: http://members.tripod.com/~Oil_Lamps/   What's Rela

Ancient Oil Lamp Reproductions

The reproduction oil lamps found on these pages represent ancient oil lamps used by the Greeks, Romans, Jews, Early Christians, Egyptians, Muslims, Syrians, North Africans, Roman-Celts, Roman-Gauls, Roman-Britians and even some early Crusaders!

The lamps are made using the traditional Roman technique pressing the raw clay into gypsum molds. The greenware is then trimmed by hand using small metal tools, and pierced with tubes, as Roman craftsman did to create the originals these copy. They are then fired to an earthenware ceramic. The resulting lamps can be used with common vegetable oil (olive oil being most favored in antiquity). A wick and instructions are provided with each lamp.

Many of the lamps are molded directly from originals. Others are styled after originals. Sizes vary, but match the range found in ancient lamps.

Unless otherwise specified in the description, most lamps are only $7.00 (US), the same low price since 1994.

For general information on ancient oil lamps check out

Lamps in Antiquity

Several of the originals pictured there have been used as a basis for the reproductions.
Coming soon- direct links to images of many of the originals used to model the reproductions!

FIGURE 2-7: A variety of ancient oil lamp reproductions are shown at this web site.

Judaism: Conservative
www.uscj.org

Judaism: Orthodox
www.ou.org

Judaism: Reconstructionist
www.jrf.org

Judaism: Reform
www.rj.org
www.uahc.org

Ner Tamid
scheinerman.net/judaism/synagogue/objects2.htm#ner

Twelve Tribes
www.hadassah.org.il/chagall.htm

Tzitzit
www.mjoe.org/ritual/tzitzit1.html
www.exo.net/bluethread/tzitzit.htm

Vegetation: Olive Trees
www.gilboa.co.il/ol-tree.htm

Vegetation: Pomegranates
www.pomegranateconnection.com/history.htm
www.tcsn.net/chadmark/pomegranate.htm

KI TISA
Exodus 30:11-34:35

Animals: Calves
www.kidsfarm.com/red.htm

Archaeology: Ancient Coins
ancient-art.com/judbib.htm
www.hum.huji.ac.il/archaeology

Art: Michelangelo's Moses (see Figure 2-8, opposite)
www.kfki.hu/~arthp/art/m/michelan/1sculptu/giulio_2/
   moses.jpg

Genizah
www.brittanica.com/seo/g/genizah

Holidays: Shabbat
www.shabat.co.il
www.jewfaq.org/shabbat.htm
www.everythingjewish.com/Shabbat/Shabbat_Origins.htm
www.ou.org/chagim/shabbat

Spice Box
www.artjudaica.com/cgi-bin/svend/gallery_havdalah
www.uahc.org/ny/tinw/ReligiousLiving/ReligiousObjects/
   HavdalahRO.htm

Figure 2-8: A photo of Michelangelo's Moses from the Web Gallery of Art. For more photos of art, go to the Web Gallery's index page at www.kfki.hu/~arthp/art/.

VAYAKHEL
Exodus 35:1-38:20

Art: Marc Chagall
www.mcs.csuhayward.edu/~malek/Chagal.html

Art: Shalom of Safed
www.sternart.com/i-shalom.htm

First Synagogue in New York
www.eldridgestreet.org

Holidays: Shabbat
www.shabat.co.il
www.jewfaq.org/shabbat.htm
www.everythingjewish.com/Shabbat/Shabbat_Origins.htm
www.ou.org/chagim/shabbat

Ketubah
www.theketubah.com

Kiddush Cup
www.mjoe.org/ritual/kiddush1.html
www.artjudaica.com/cgi-bin/svend/gallery_kiddish

Maps: Ancient Israel
www.wsu.edu/~dee/HEBREWS/ANISRMAP.HTM

Megillah
207.168.91.4/vjholidays/purim/readmeg.htm

Menorah

www.templeinstitute.org/vessels/menorah.html

Tallit (see Figure 2-9, below)

www.mjoe.org/ritual/tallit1.html

www.artjudaica.com/cgi-bin/svend/gallery_tallit

Figure 2-9: This web site contains information about various ritual objects, including the *tallit*.

Vegetation: Acacia Trees

www.anbg.gov.au/acacia

PIKUDAY
Exodus 38:21-40:38

Calendar – Jewish

www.jewfaq.org/calendar.html

kids.infoplease.lycos.com/ipka/a0777385.html

bnaibrith.org/caln.html

Maps: Ancient Middle East

www.khouse.org/blueletter/images/maps/Otest/world.jpg

Organizations: Habitat for Humanity (see Figure 2-10, opposite)

www.habitat.org

Synagogues

www.mlandau-architects.com/synagogue.htm

Tallit

www.mjoe.org/ritual/tallit1.html

www.artjudaica.com/cgi-bin/svend/gallery_tallit

Figure 2-10: Home page for HABITAT FOR HUMANITY

LEVITICUS

VAYIKRA
Leviticus 1:1-5:26

Animals: Birds (see Figure 3-1, below)
members.aol.com/zoonet/pictures/mourningdove.jpg

FIGURE 3-1: This screen shot is representative of the thousands of animal photos that can be found on the Internet.

Animals: Bulls

www.angus.com
www.kidsfarm.com/bull.htm

Animals: Cows

www.mindspring.com/~zoonet/barnyard/pictures/cow.jpg

Animals: Goats

members.aol.com/zoonet/pictures/angoragoat.jpg

Animals: Rams

raysweb.net/wildlife/pages/02.html

Animals: Sheep

www.mindspring.com/~zoonet/pinemoun/pictures/sheep.jpg

Challah

www.bus.ualberta.ca/yreshef/shabbat/shabcustoms.html
biblicalholidays.com/Sabbath/challah.htm

Egypt: Ancient Culture

emuseum.mankato.msus.edu/prehistory/egypt/history/
history.html

Matzah

aish.com/holidays/passover/articles/immediate_changes.asp
graphicdesign.miningco.com/arts/graphicdesign/library/
passover/blpasclip1.htm

Mikvah

www.his.com/~chabad/Mikvah.htm

Sacrifices

www.templeinstitute.org/services/Sacrifices.html

Shabbat Candles

www.ucalgary.ca/~elsegal/Shokel/951102_Two_Candles.html

Wrongdoing by Public Officials

www.villagevice.com

TZAV
Leviticus 6:1-8:36

Animals: Birds

members.aol.com/zoonet/pictures/mourningdove.jpg

Animals: Bulls

www.angus.com
www.kidsfarm.com/bull.htm

Animals: Cows

www.mindspring.com/~zoonet/barnyard/pictures/cow.jpg

Animals: Goats (see Figure 3-2, opposite)

members.aol.com/zoonet/pictures/angoragoat.jpg

Animals: Rams

raysweb.net/wildlife/pages/02.html

Location: http://members.aol.com/zoonet/pictures/angoragoat.jpg   What's Re

Pine Mountain Wild Animal Park   Angora Goat   ©1996 ZooNet™

FIGURE 3-2: Yet another animal photo that can be found on the Internet. Goats were important to the ancient Israelites, providing milk, wool, and meat. Goats were also used for sacrifice.

Animals: Sheep

www.mindspring.com/~zoonet/pinemoun/pictures/sheep.jpg

Judaism: Conservative

www.uscj.org

Judaism: Orthodox

www.ou.org

Judaism: Reconstructionist
www.jrf.org

Judaism: Reform
www.rj.org
www.uahc.org

Kashrut
www.kashrut.com
www.kosherfinder.com

SHEMINI
Leviticus 9:1-11:47

Animals: Cows
www.mindspring.com/~zoonet/barnyard/pictures/cow.jpg

Animals: Goats
members.aol.com/zoonet/pictures/angoragoat.jpg

Animals: Pigs
members.tripod.lycos.nl/piggies

Kashrut (see Figure 3-3, opposite)
www.kashrut.com
www.kosherfinder.com

FIGURE 3-3: The KOSHERFINDER home page claims to be
"your guide to everything kosher."

Religions: Buddhism

www.ncf.carleton.ca/dharma/introduction/buddhism.html
buddhism.about.com/religion/buddhism/blbud101.htm

Religions: Hinduism
www.geocities.com/RodeoDrive/1415/indexd.html
www.holyindia.org

Religions: Islam
www.iad.org/intro/intro.html

TAZRIA
Leviticus 12:1-13:59

Handicapped (see Figure 3-4, opposite)
www.geocities.com/Athens/4611
www.usdoj.gov/crt/ada/adahom1.htm

Leprosy (Hansen's Disease)
www.who.int/lep
www.cdc.gov/ncidod/dbmd/diseaseinfo/hansens_t.htm

METZORA
Leviticus 14:1-15:33

Animals: Birds
members.aol.com/zoonet/pictures/mourningdove.jpg

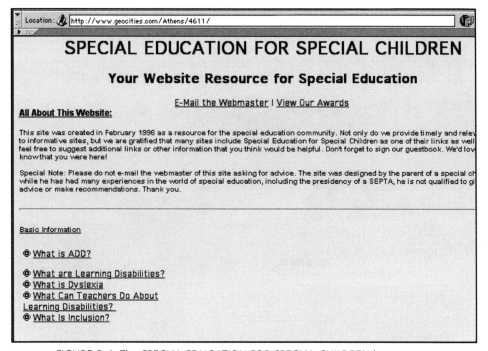

Location: http://www.geocities.com/Athens/4611/

SPECIAL EDUCATION FOR SPECIAL CHILDREN

Your Website Resource for Special Education

E-Mail the Webmaster | View Our Awards

All About This Website:

This site was created in February 1996 as a resource for the special education community. Not only do we provide timely and relev to informative sites, but we are gratified that many sites include Special Education for Special Children as one of their links as well feel free to suggest additional links or other information that you think would be helpful. Don't forget to sign our guestbook. We'd lov knowthat you were here!

Special Note: Please do not e-mail the webmaster of this site asking for advice. The site was designed by the parent of a special ch while he has had many experiences in the world of special education, including the presidency of a SEPTA, he is not qualified to gi advice or make recommendations. Thank you.

Basic Information

◉ What is ADD?

◉ What are Learning Disabilities?
◉ What is Dyslexia
◉ What Can Teachers Do About
Learning Disabilities?
◉ What Is Inclusion?

FIGURE 3-4: The SPECIAL EDUCATION FOR SPECIAL CHILDREN home page.

Animals: Crimson Worm

www.templeinstitute.org/vessels/priestly-garments.html

Handicapped

www.geocities.com/Athens/4611

www.usdoj.gov/crt/ada/adahom1.htm

Leprosy (Hansen's Disease)

www.who.int/lep

www.cdc.gov/ncidod/dbmd/diseaseinfo/hansens_t.htm

Mikvah

www.his.com/~chabad/Mikvah.htm

Organizations: AIDS Organizations (see Figure 3-5, below)

www.thebody.com/help.html

FIGURE 3-5: A portion of THE BODY home page, from which you can link to more than 60 AIDS-related resources.

Vegetation: Cedar Wood

www.orst.edu/instruct/for241/con/trcedgen.html

Vegetation: Hyssop (moss)

www.chatlink.com/~herbseed/hyssop.htm

ACHARAY MOT
Leviticus 16:1-18:30

Animals: Goats
members.aol.com/zoonet/pictures/angoragoat.jpg

Egypt: Ancient Culture
emuseum.mankato.msus.edu/prehistory/egypt/history/
history.html

Holidays: Yom Kippur (see Figure 3-6, page 52)
207.168.91.4/vjholidays/rosh/yomstep.htm
www.holidays.net/highholydays

Kashrut
www.kashrut.com
www.kosherfinder.com

KEDOSHIM
Leviticus 19:1-20:27

Biographies: Modern Individuals
amillionlives.com

Holidays: Shabbat
www.shabat.co.il
www.jewfaq.org/shabbat.htm
www.everythingjewish.com/Shabbat/Shabbat_Origins.htm
www.ou.org/chagim/shabbat

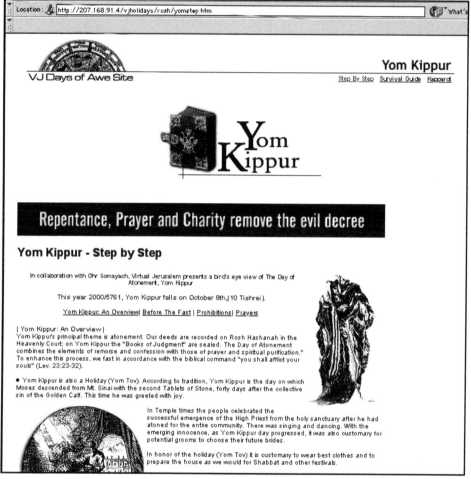

FIGURE 3-6: A portion of the Yom Kippur web page found
on the VIRTUAL JERUSALEM web site.

Organizations: Jewish Braille Institute
www.jewishbraille.org

Organizations: Local Tzedakah Opportunities
(see Figure 3-7, opposite)
www.volunteermatch.org

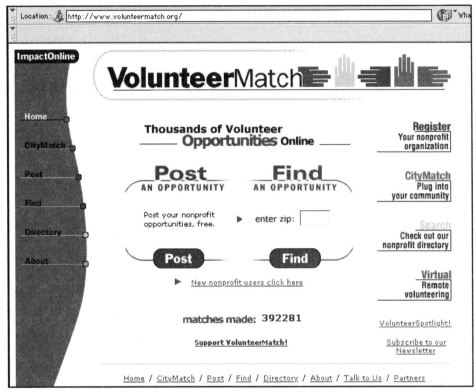

FIGURE 3-7: The VOLUNTEER MATCH web site is a locator service that helps volunteers find service opportunities.

Organizations: National Congress of the Jewish Deaf (Jewish deaf links)

www.jdcc.org/links/links.html

Synagogues

www.mlandau-architects.com/synagogue.htm

EMOR
Leviticus 21:1-24:23

Calendar – Jewish
www.jewfaq.org/calendar.html
kids.infoplease.lycos.com/ipka/a0777385.html
bnaibrith.org/caln.html

Etrog
207/168.91.4/vjholidays/sukkot/minim.htm

Holidays: Passover
207.168.91.4/vjholidays/pesach/Home.htm
www.holidays.net/passover

Holidays: Rosh HaShanah
207.168.91.4/vjholidays/rosh/index.htm
www.holidays.net/highholydays

Holidays: Shabbat
www.shabat.co.il
www.jewfaq.org/shabbat.htm
www.everythingjewish.com/Shabbat/Shabbat_Origins.htm
www.ou.org/chagim/shabbat

Holidays: Shavuot
207.168.91.4/vjholidays/shavuot
www.holidays.net/shavuot

Holidays: Sukkot
207.168.91.4/vjholidays/sukkot
www.holidays.net/sukkot

Holidays: Yom Kippur
207.168.91.4/vjholidays/rosh/yom.htm
www.holidays.net/highholydays

Lulav
207.168.91.4/vjholidays/sukkot/minim.htm

Shofar
www.holidays.net/highholydays/shofar.htm
www.judaicaonline.com/CT_Misc/PRMS2_MSG427.htm

Vegetation: Olive Trees (see Figure 3-8, page 56)
www.gilboa.co.il/ol-tree.htm

BEHAR
Leviticus 25:1-26:2

Holidays: Shabbat
www.shabat.co.il
www.jewfaq.org/shabbat.htm
www.everythingjewish.com/Shabbat/Shabbat_Origins.htm
www.ou.org/chagim/shabbat

Holidays: Yom Kippur

207.168.91.4/vjholidays/rosh/yom.htm

www.holidays.net/highholydays

Liberty Bell (see Figure 3-9, opposite)

www.nps.gov/inde/liberty-bell.html

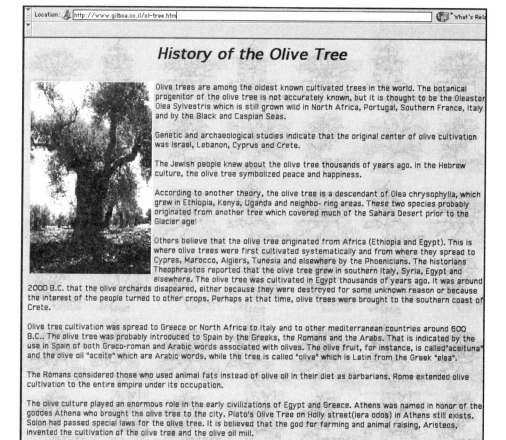

FIGURE 3-8: According to this web page, the olive tree symbolized
peace and happiness in the Hebrew culture.

Organizations: Jewish National Fund
www.jnf.org

Netsite: http://www.nps.gov/inde/liberty-bell.htm   What's Rela

Liberty Bell

Market Street between 5th and 6th Streets.

"Proclaim liberty throughout all the land unto all the inhabitants thereof - Lev. XXV, v. x. By order of the Assembly of the Province of Pensylvania [sic] for the State House in Philada."

Liberty Bell Inscription

Visiting

The Liberty Bell pavilion is located on Market Street between 5th and 6th Streets. The building is open year round, though <u>hours</u> vary by season.

Talks about the Liberty Bell are presented continuously. Audio tapes can be played on request in 16 foreign languages. After hours the Bell may be seen through a glass viewing window, where visitors may play a tape explaining the bell's story.

The Bell's Message

The Liberty Bell's inscription conveys a message of liberty which goes beyond the words themselves. Since the bell was made, the words of the inscription have meant different things to different people.

When William Penn created Pennsylvania's government he allowed citizens to take part in making laws and gave them the right to choose the religion they wanted. The colonists were proud of the freedom that Penn gave them. In 1751, the Speaker of the Pennsylvania Assembly ordered a new bell for the State House. He asked that a Bible verse to be placed on the bell - "Proclaim LIBERTY throughout all the Land unto all the inhabitants thereof" (Leviticus 25:10). As the official bell of the Pennsylvania State House (today called Independence Hall) it rang many times for public announcements, but we remember times like July 8, 1776 when it rang to announce the first public reading of the Declaration of Independence.

The old State House bell was first called the "Liberty Bell" by a group trying to outlaw slavery. These abolitionists remembered the words on the bell and, in the 1830s, adopted it as a symbol of their cause.

Beginning in the late 1800s, the Liberty Bell travelled around the country to expositions and fairs to help heal the divisions of the Civil War. It reminded Americans of their earlier days when they fought and worked together for independence.

In 1915, the bell made its last trip and came home to Philadelphia, where it now silently reminds us of the power of liberty. For more than 200 years people from around the world have felt the bell's message. No one can see liberty, but people have used the Liberty Bell to represent this important idea.

FIGURE 3-9: This portion of The Liberty Bell web page is part of the NATIONAL PARK SERVICE web site.

BECHUKOTAI
Leviticus 26:3-27:34

Holidays: Rosh HaShanah (see Figure 3-10, below)
207.168.91.4/vjholidays/rosh/index.htm
www.holidays.net/highholydays

FIGURE 3-10: The Rosh HaShanah web page is yet another holiday-related resource on the VIRTUAL JERUSALEM web site.

Holidays: Yom Kippur

207.168.91.4/vjholidays/rosh/yom.htm

www.holidays.net/highholydays

NUMBERS

BAMIDBAR
Numbers 1:1-4:20

Maps: Sinai (see Figure 4-1, below)
www.khouse.org/blueletter/images/maps/Otest/sinai.gif

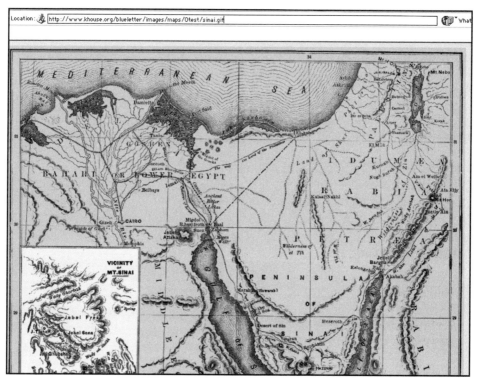

FIGURE 4-1: A portion of a web page showing a map of the Sinai region.

Organizations: North American Conference on Ethiopian Jewry
www.circus.org/nacoej.htm

Twelve Tribes
www.hadassah.org.il/chagall.htm

U.S. Census Bureau
www.census.gov

NASO
Numbers 4:21-7:89

Holidays: Shabbat (see Figure 4-2, page 62)
www.shabat.co.il
www.jewfaq.org/shabbat.htm
www.everythingjewish.com/Shabbat/Shabbat_Origins.htm
www.ou.org/chagim/shabbat

Judaism: Conservative
www.uscj.org

Judaism: Orthodox
www.ou.org

Judaism: Reconstructionist
www.jrf.org

FIGURE 4-2: Home page of THE ULTIMATE SHABBAT SITE.

Judaism: Reform

www.rj.org

www.uahc.org

Kiddush Cup

www.mjoe.org/ritual/kiddush1.html

www.artjudaica.com/cgi-bin/svend/gallery_kiddish

Twelve Tribes

www.hadassah.org.il/chagall.htm

BEHA'ALOTECHA
Numbers 8:1-12:16

Animals: Quail
www.ngpc.state.ne.us/wildlife/quail.html

Archaeology: Ancient Trumpets (see Figure 4-3, below)
www.christianfloral.com/stamps/instruments.htm

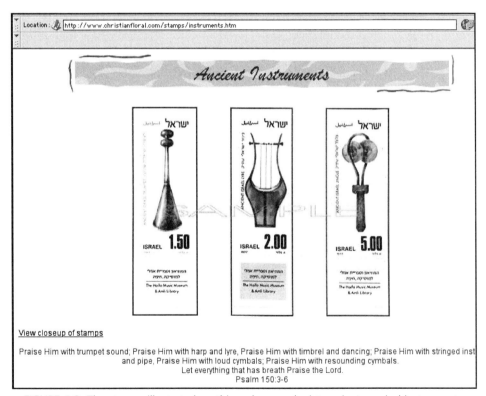

FIGURE 4-3: The stamps illustrated on this web page depict ancient musical instruments.

Holidays: Passover

207.168.91.4/vjholidays/pesach/Home.htm

www.holidays.net/passover

Leprosy (Hansen's Disease)

www.who.int/lep

www.cdc.gov/ncidod/dbmd/diseaseinfo/hansens_t.htm

Maps: Sinai

www.khouse.org/blueletter/images/maps/Otest/sinai.gif

Menorah

www.templeinstitute.org/vessels/menorah.html

Organizations: Jewish Healing Center

www.growthhouse.org/ruachami.html

SHELACH LECHA
Numbers 13:1-15:41

Challah

www.bus.ualberta.ca/yreshef/shabbat/shabcustoms.html

biblicalholidays.com/Sabbath/challah.htm

Holidays: Tisha B'Av (see Figure 4-4, opposite)

207.168.91.4/vjholidays/3weeks

FIGURE 4-4: A web page devoted to the Three Weeks of mourning
that lead up to the fast of Tisha B'Av.

Maps: Ancient Israel
www.wsu.edu/~dee/HEBREWS/ANISRMAP.HTM

Tallit
www.mjoe.org/ritual/tallit1.html
www.artjudaica.com/cgi-bin/svend/gallery_tallit

Twelve Tribes
www.hadassah.org.il/chagall.htm

Vegetation: Grapes
osu.orst.edu/food-resource/images/FRUITVEG/GRAPES/
   on_vine(ac).jpg
wine.about.com/food/wine/library/encyc/bl_grapes_primer/.htm

KORACH
Numbers 16:1-18:32

Aliyah
www.wzo.org.il/aliyah/index.html

Pidyon HaBen
www.us-israel.org/jsource/Judaism/Pidyon_Haben.html

Salt (see Figure 4-5, opposite)
www.saltinfo.com

Twelve Tribes
www.hadassah.org.il/chagall.htm

CHUKAT
Numbers 19:1-22:1

American Medical Association (AMA) – Symbol
www.ama-assn.org
encarta.msn.com/find/Concise.asp?ti=01478000

Animals: Bulls
www.angus.com
www.kidsfarm.com/bull.htm

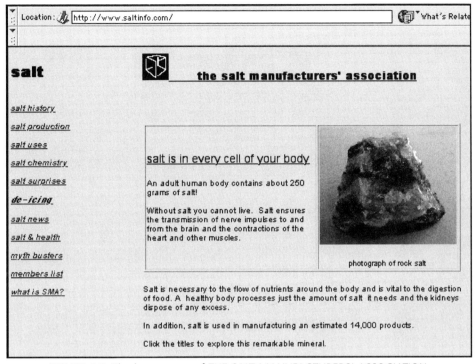

FIGURE 4-5: The home page of THE SALT MANUFACTURERS' ASSOCIATION.

Animals: Snakes
www.snakeworld.com

www.wnybiz.com/markheim/reptile/pic32.jpg

Maps: Ancient Israel
www.wsu.edu/~dee/HEBREWS/ANISRMAP.HTM

Organizations: Coalition on the Environment and Jewish Life
(see Figure 4-6, page 68)

www.coejl.org

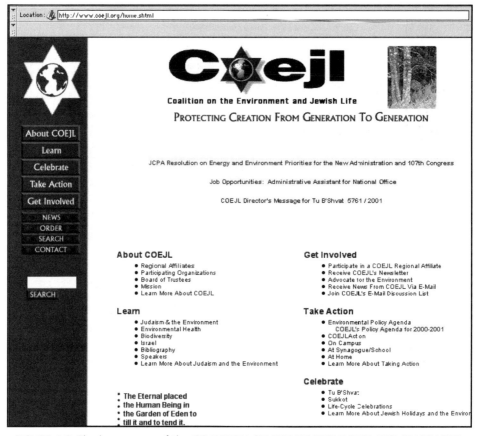

FIGURE 4-6: The home page of the COALITION ON THE ENVIRONMENT AND JEWISH LIFE.

BALAK
Numbers 22:2-25:9

Animals: Donkeys (see Figure 4-7, opposite)
www.mindspring.com/~zoonet/barnyard/pictures/donkey.jpg

Falashas
www.geocities.com/CollegePark/7139

Location: http://www.mindspring.com/~zoonet/barnyard/pictures/donkey.jpg

Donkey   ©1995 ZooNet™

FIGURE 4-7: This donkey is yet another example of the fine animal photos found on the ZOONET web site.

Maps: Ancient Israel
www.wsu.edu/~dee/HEBREWS/ANISRMAP.HTM

Organizations: North American Conference on Ethiopian Jewry
www.circus.org/nacoej.htm

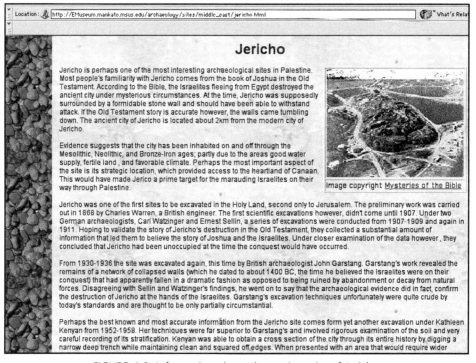

FIGURE 4-8: Information about the ancient city of Jericho
found on the EMUSEUM web site.

PINCHAS
Numbers 25:10-30:1

Archaeology: Jericho (see Figure 4-8, above)
 EMuseum.mankato.msus.edu/archaeology/sites/
  middle_east/jericho.html

Holidays: Passover
 207.168.91.4/vjholidays/pesach/Home.htm
 www.holidays.net/passover

Holidays: Rosh Chodesh

www.bus.ualberta.ca/yreshef/shabbat/roshframes.html

Holidays: Rosh HaShanah

207.168.91.4/vjholidays/rosh/index.htm

www.holidays.net/highholydays

Holidays: Shabbat

www.shabat.co.il

www.jewfaq.org/shabbat.htm

www.everythingjewish.com/Shabbat/Shabbat_Origins.htm

www.ou.org/chagim/shabbat

Holidays: Shavuot

207.168.91.4/vjholidays/shavuot

www.holidays.net/shavuot

Holidays: Sukkot

207.168.91.4/vjholidays/sukkot

www.holidays.net/sukkot

Holidays: Yom Kippur

207.168.91.4/vjholidays/rosh/yom.htm

www.holidays.net/highholydays

Maps: Ancient Israel

www.wsu.edu/~dee/HEBREWS/ANISRMAP.HTM

Organizations: Redistribution Center

www.ziv.org/ziv99_annprt2.html

Vegetation: Fig Trees
aggie-horticulture.tamu.edu/extension/homefruit/fig/fig.html

MATOT
Numbers 30:2-32:42

Archaeology: Jericho
EMuseum.mankato.msus.edu/archaeology/sites/
  middle_east/jericho.html

Holidays: Yom Kippur
207.168.91.4/vjholidays/rosh/yom.htm
www.holidays.net/highholydays

Jordan River
encarta.msn.com/find/Concise.asp?ti=06512000

Maps: Ancient Israel
www.wsu.edu/~dee/HEBREWS/ANISRMAP.HTM

Maps: Twelve Tribes
www.khouse.org/blueletter/images/maps/Otest/boundaries.gif

Organizations: New Israel Fund (see Figure 4-9, opposite)
www.nif.org/home

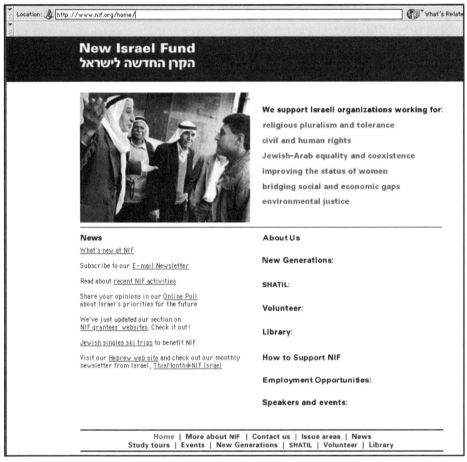

FIGURE 4-9: Home page of the NEW ISRAEL FUND.

MAS'AY
Numbers 33:1-36:13

Archaeology: Jericho
EMuseum.mankato.msus.edu/archaeology/sites/
middle_east/jericho.html

Holidays: Shabbat

www.jewfaq.org/shabbat.htm
www.everythingjewish.com/Shabbat/Shabbat_Origins.htm
www.ou.org/chagim/shabbat
www.shabat.co.il

Maps: Ancient Israel

www.wsu.edu/~dee/HEBREWS/ANISRMAP.HTM

Maps: Cities of Refuge (see Figure 4-10, opposite)

www.khouse.org/blueletter/images/maps/Otest/refuge.html

Maps: Modern Israel

www.lib.utexas.edu/Libs/PCL/Map_collection/
    middle_east_and_asia/Israel.GIF

Maps: Sinai

www.khouse.org/blueletter/images/maps/Otest/sinai.gif

Maps: Twelve Tribes

www.khouse.org/blueletter/images/maps/Otest/boundaries.gif

Suffrage Movement

www.pbs.org/onewoman/suffrage.html

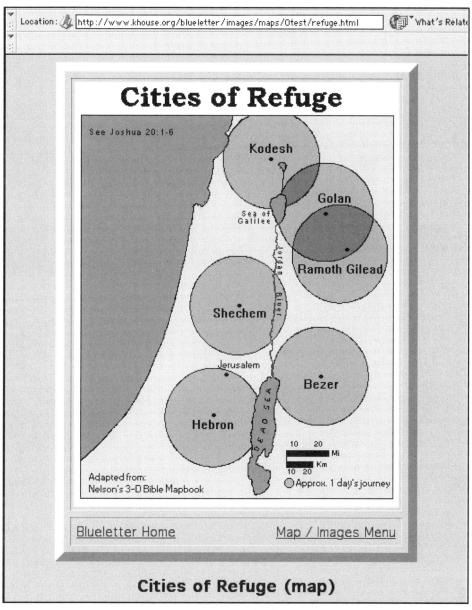

Location: http://www.khouse.org/blueletter/images/maps/Otest/refuge.html   What's Relate

Cities of Refuge

See Joshua 20:1-6

Kodesh

Golan

Sea of
Galilee

Ramoth Gilead

Shechem

Jerusalem

Bezer

Hebron

10   20
Mi
Km
10   20

Adapted from:
Nelson's 3-D Bible Mapbook

Approx. 1 day's journey

Blueletter Home   Map / Images Menu

Cities of Refuge (map)

FIGURE 4-10: A map showing the Cities of Refuge as mentioned in Numbers.

DEUTERONOMY

DEVARIM
Deuteronomy 1:1-3:22

Animals: Bees
www.beekeeping.com/info/sommaires/index_us.html
fly.hiwaay.net/~btucker/gifs/animals/bumblebe.gif

Holidays: Passover
207.168.91.4/vjholidays/pesach/Home.htm
www.holidays.net/passover

Mahatma Ghandi Speeches
www.mkgandhi.org/quots.htm

Maps: Ancient Israel
www.wsu.edu/~dee/HEBREWS/ANISRMAP.HTM

Maps: Sinai
www.khouse.org/blueletter/images/maps/Otest/sinai.gif

Martin Luther King, Jr.: "I Have a Dream" Speech
web66.coled.umn.edu/new/MLK/MLK.html

Organizations: American Jewish Archives
huc.edu/aja

Organizations: American Jewish Historical Society
www.ajhs.org

Organizations: U.S. Holocaust Memorial Council
(see Figure 5-1, below)
www.ushmm.org

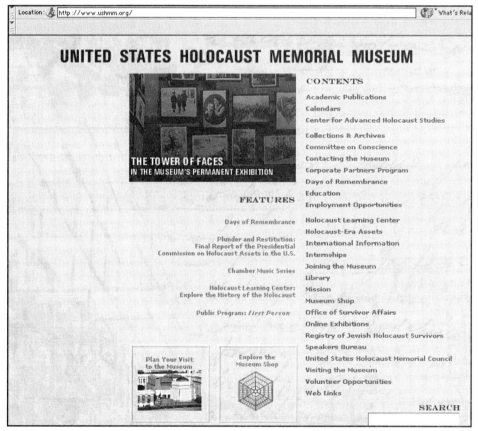

FIGURE 5-1: Home page of the UNITED STATES HOLOCAUST MEMORIAL MUSEUM.

Organizations: YIVO Institute for Jewish Research
www.yivoinstitute.org

U.S. Judicial System
encarta.msn.com/find/Concise.asp?ti=06747000
www.firstgov.gov/us_gov/judicial_branch.html

Yitzhak Rabin Speeches
www.ariga.com/peacebiz/rabin/lastrabn.htm

Zionists – Early Chalutzim
www.jajz-ed.org.il/100/time/index.html

VA'ETCHANAN
Deuteronomy 3:23-7:11

Holidays: Shabbat
www.jewfaq.org/shabbat.htm
www.everythingjewish.com/Shabbat/Shabbat_Origins.htm
www.ou.org/chagim/shabbat
www.shabat.co.il

Holidays: Tisha B'Av
207.168.91.4/vjholidays/3weeks

Jerusalem (see Figure 5-2, opposite)
www.us-israel.org/jsource/vie/Jerutoc.html

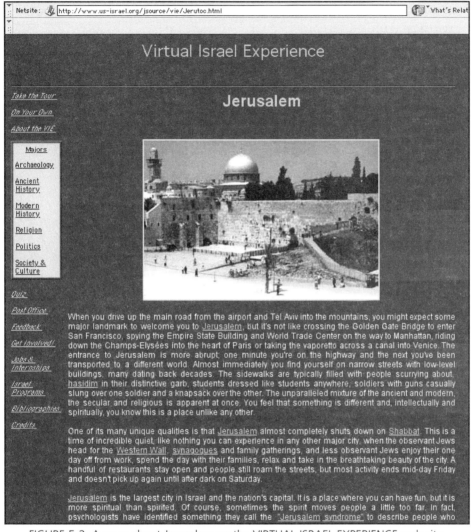

FIGURE 5-2: A page about Jerusalem on the VIRTUAL ISRAEL EXPERIENCE web site.

Maps: Ancient Israel

www.wsu.edu/~dee/HEBREWS/ANISRMAP.HTM

Mezzuzah

www.nvo.com/menshenables/mezzuzot

Tefillin (see Figure 5-3, opposite)

www.tefillin.co.il

www.mjoe.org/ritual/tefillin1.html

EKEV
Deuteronomy 7:12-11:25

Jerusalem

www.us-israel.org/jsource/vie/Jerutoc.html

Jordan River

encarta.msn.com/find/Concise.asp?ti=06512000

Maps: Ancient Israel

www.wsu.edu/~dee/HEBREWS/ANISRMAP.HTM

Organizations: MAZON

www.mazon.org

Tefillin

www.tefillin.co.il

www.mjoe.org/ritual/tefillin1.html

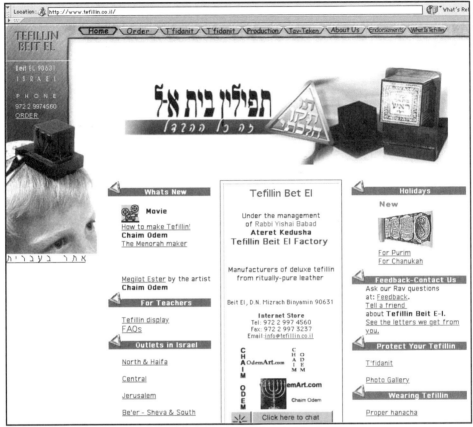

FIGURE 5-3: A web page devoted to *tefillin*.

RE'EH
Deuteronomy 11:26-16:17

Archaeology: A Tel (see Figure 5-4, page 82)
www.tau.ac.il/~archpubs/megiddo/index.html

Blood Libel
www.fordham.edu/halsall/source/rinn.html

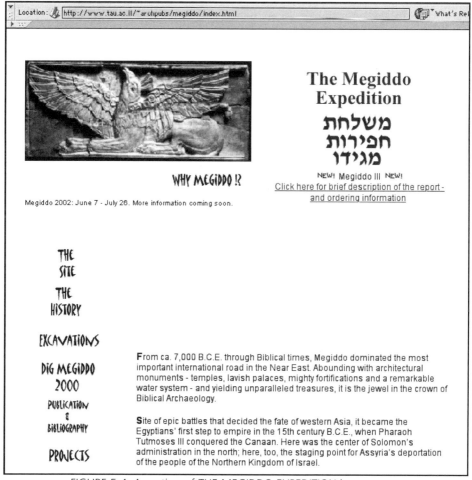

FIGURE 5-4: A portion of THE MEGIDDO EXPEDITION home page.

Genizah
www.brittanica.com/seo/g/genizah

Holidays: Passover
207.168.91.4/vjholidays/pesach/Home.htm
www.holidays.net/passover

Holidays: Shavuot
207.168.91.4/vjholidays/shavuot

www.holidays.net/shavuot

Holidays: Sukkot
207.168.91.4/vjholidays/sukkot

www.holidays.net/sukkot

Jerusalem
www.us-israel.org/jsource/vie/Jerutoc.html

Kashrut
www.kashrut.com

www.kosherfinder.com

Maps: Modern Israel
www.lib.utexas.edu/Libs/PCL/Map_collection/
middle_east_and_asia/Israel.GIF

Organizations: National Conference for Community and Justice (formerly the National Conference of Christians and Jews)
www.nccj.org

Shabbatai Zvi
www.us-israel.org/jsource/biography/Zvi.html

U.S. Civil War – Slavery
www.iath.virginia.edu/utc/sitemap.html

www.jewish-history.com/civilwar.htm

SHOFETIM
Deuteronomy 16:18-21:9

Bet Alpha Synagogue in Israel – Zodiac Floor
www.hefzi.org.il/turism/betsynagogue.html
ccat.sas.upenn.edu/rs/2/Judaism/bethalpha.htm

Justice Symbol (see Figure 5-5, opposite)
www.dejohnson.com/scalesofjustice.html

Kashrut
www.kashrut.com
www.kosherfinder.com

Maps: Ancient Israel
www.wsu.edu/~dee/HEBREWS/ANISRMAP.HTM

Organizations: Jewish National Fund
www.jnf.org

Vegetation: Cedar Trees
www.orst.edu/instruct/for241/con/trcedgen.html

Vegetation: Cypress Trees
www.orst.edu/instruct/for241/con/cyprgen.html

Vegetation: Fruit Bearing Trees
www.virtualorchard.net

Vegetation: Non-fruit Bearing Trees
www.orst.edu/instruct/for241/con/trcedgen.html

FIGURE 5-5: This Scales of Justice figure is a familiar symbol of impartiality and fairness.

Weddings
www.ohr.org.il/judaism/articles/wedding.htm

KI TAYTZAY
Deuteronomy 21:10-25:19

Amalek
aish.com/holidays/purim/haman_heir_to_amalek.asp

Animals: Bird with Young
eelink.net/EndSpp/ESimages/leastter.GIF
http://birding.about.com/hobbies/birding/msub43-baby.htm

Animals: Donkeys
www.mindspring.com/~zoonet/barnyard/pictures/donkey.jpg

Animals: Oxen
members.aol.com/zoonet/pictures/gaur.jpg

Get (Jewish Divorce)
www.ahavat-israel.com/torat/divorce.asp

Holidays: Purim
207.168.91.4/vjholidays/purim/index.htm
www.holidays.net/purim

Judaism: Conservative
www.uscj.org

Judaism: Orthodox
www.ou.org

Judaism: Reconstructionist
www.jrf.org

Judaism: Reform
www.rj.org
www.uahc.org

Mezzuzah
www.nvo.com/menshenables/mezzuzot

Organizations: Birds of Prey Foundation
www.birds-of-prey.org

Organizations: Horse Protection League
www.hpl-colo.org

Parapet/Roof (see Figure 5-6, page 88)
architecture.about.com/arts/architecture/library/
blgloss-parapet.htm

Shakespeare
tech-two.mit.edu/Shakespeare/works.html

Tzitzit
www.mjoe.org/ritual/tzitzit1.html
www.exo.net/bluethread/tzitzit.htm

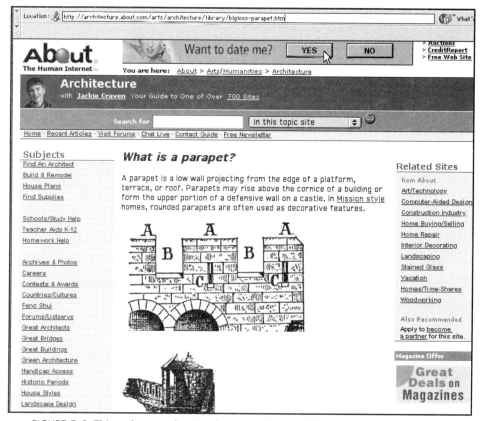

FIGURE 5-6: This web page about architecture includes information about parapets.

KI TAVO
Deuteronomy 26:1-29:8

Holidays: Passover (see Figure 5-7, opposite)
207.168.91.4/vjholidays/pesach/Home.htm
www.holidays.net/passover

Maps: Ancient Israel
www.wsu.edu/~dee/HEBREWS/ANISRMAP.HTM

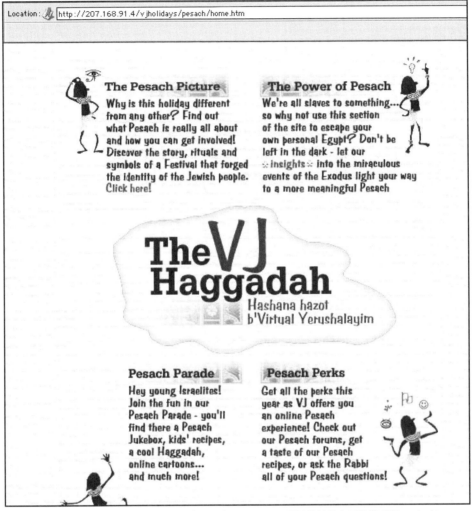

FIGURE 5-7: A page about Pesach on the VIRTUAL JERUSALEM HOLIDAYS web site.

Twelve Tribes

www.hadassah.org.il/chagall.htm

U.S. Taxation

www.firstgov.gov/topics/money.html

NITZAVIM
Deuteronomy 29:9-30:20

Holidays: Rosh HaShanah
207.168.91.4/vjholidays/rosh/index.htm
www.holidays.net/highholydays

Holidays: Yom Kippur
207.168.91.4/vjholidays/rosh/yom.htm
www.holidays.net/highholydays

Judaism: Reform
www.rj.org
www.uahc.org

Organizations: World Union for Progressive Judaism
rj.org/wupj

Shofar (see Figure 5-8, opposite)
www.holidays.net/highholydays/shofar.htm
www.judaicaonline.com/CT_Misc/PRMS2_MSG427.htm

VAYAYLECH
Deuteronomy 31:1-30

Holidays: Sukkot
207.168.91.4/vjholidays/sukkot
www.holidays.net/sukkot

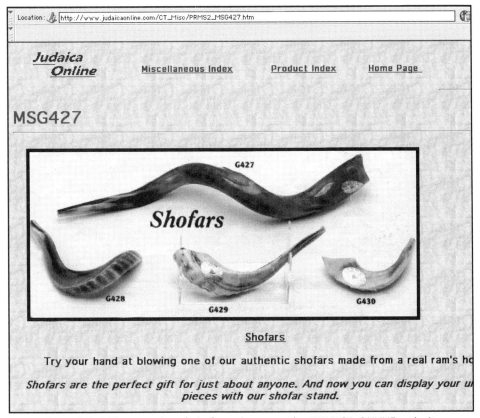

FIGURE 5-8: Different styles of *shofarot* shown on the JUDAICA ONLINE web site.

Shofar

www.holidays.net/highholydays/shofar.htm

www.judaicaonline.com/CT_Misc/PRMS2_MSG427.htm

Sofer (Torah Scribe) (see Figure 5-9, page 92)

www.thesoferstam.com/about_the_sofer.htm

www.neilyerman.com

FIGURE 5-9: A modern day Torah scribe or *sofer*.

HA'AZINU
Deuteronomy 32:1-52

Holidays: Chanukah (see Figure 5-10, opposite)
   207.168.91.4/vjholidays/chanukah/index.htm

FIGURE 5-10: The Chanukah web page at the VIRTUAL JERUSALEM HOLIDAYS web site.

Maps: Ancient Israel

www.wsu.edu/~dee/HEBREWS/ANISRMAP.HTM

Vegetation: Grapes

osu.orst.edu/food-resource/images/FRUITVEG/GRAPES/
on_vine(ac).jpg

wine.about.com/food/wine/library/encyc/bl_grapes_primer/.htm

Vegetation: Olive Trees

www.gilboa.co.il/ol-tree.htm

Vegetation: Wheat
www.crop.cri.nz/foodinfo/millbake/whgrain.htm

V'ZOT HABRACHAH
Deuteronomy 33:1-34:12

Holidays: Simchat Torah (see Figure 5-11, opposite)
207.168.91.4/vjholidays/simchatorah

Maps: Ancient Israel
www.wsu.edu/~dee/HEBREWS/ANISRMAP.HTM

Twelve Tribes
www.hadassah.org.il/chagall.htm

Yahrzeit
www.yahrzeit.org/yizkor.html

FIGURE 5-11: The Simchat Torah page at the VIRTUAL JERUSALEM HOLIDAYS web site.
(Note: The image above is what you will see when using the Microsoft Internet
Explorer browser. When using Netscape Navigator browser, the scroll
is closed and does not open until you click on it.)

Part II:
Internet Resources by Topic

The material in this section is most valuable for those not using *Teaching Torah*, but who are incorporating a different curriculum as they teach Torah. As you come to a new topic of interest, refer to this section to see what Internet resources are available for enhancing your curriculum.

Although most of the items are simply arranged alphabetically, a number of subject areas have been grouped together. These include:

- Animals
- Art
- Judaism (denominations)
- Holidays
- Maps
- Organizations (Jewish and secular, which on an everyday basis deal with the concepts promoted in the Torah)
- Religions (non–Jewish)
- Vegetation

The Internet sites in this section are arranged alphabetically by topic. The Torah portions to which the material at a particular site is most applicable are also listed. Some sites may contain other material that is applicable to Torah portions not listed specifically in this section.

Again, remember that not every single item or topic can be found on the Internet. However, if you have trouble finding material on a particular topic, refer to "What to Do If Something Can't Be Found Online" (page xix) for tips on how to discover online resources quickly.

Aliyah

www.wzo.org.il/aliyah/index.html

Applicable Portion: KORACH – Numbers 16:1-18:32

Amalek

aish.com/holidays/purim/haman_heir_to_amalek.asp

Applicable Portions: VAYISHLACH – Genesis 32:4-36:43

BESHALACH – Exodus 13:17-17:16

KI TAYTZAY – Deuteronomy 21:10-25:19

American Medical Association (AMA) – Symbol

www.ama-assn.org

encarta.msn.com/find/Concise.asp?ti=01478000

Applicable Portion: CHUKAT – Numbers 19:1-22:1

Animals: Bees

www.beekeeping.com/info/sommaires/index_us.html

fly.hiwaay.net/~btucker/gifs/animals/bumblebe.gif

Applicable Portion: DEVARIM – Deuteronomy 1:1-3:22

Animals: Bird with Young

eelink.net/EndSpp/ESimages/leastter.GIF

http://birding.about.com/hobbies/birding/msub43-baby.htm

Applicable Portion: KI TAYTZAY – Deuteronomy 21:10-25:19

Animals: Birds

members.aol.com/zoonet/pictures/mourningdove.jpg

Applicable Portions: VAYIKRA – Leviticus 1:1-5:26

TZAV – Leviticus 6:1-8:36

METZORA – Leviticus 14:1-15:33

Animals: Bulls

www.angus.com

www.kidsfarm.com/bull.htm

Applicable Portions: VAYIKRA – Leviticus 1:1-5:26

                        TZAV – Leviticus 6:1-8:36

                        CHUKAT – Numbers 19:1-22:1

Animals: Calves

www.kidsfarm.com/red.htm

Applicable Portions: TERUMAH – Exodus 25:1-27:19

                        KI TISA – Exodus 30:11-34:35

Animals: Cows

www.mindspring.com/~zoonet/barnyard/pictures/cow.jpg

Applicable Portions: VAYIKRA – Leviticus 1:1-5:26

                        TZAV – Leviticus 6:1-8:36

                        SHEMINI – Leviticus 9:1-11:47

Animals: Crimson Worm

www.templeinstitute.org/vessels/priestly–garments.html

Applicable Portion: METZORA - Leviticus 14:1-15:33

Animals: Donkeys

www.mindspring.com/~zoonet/barnyard/pictures/donkey.jpg

Applicable Portions: BALAK – Numbers 22:2-25:9

                        KI TAYTZAY – Deuteronomy 21:10-25:19

Animals: Goats

members.aol.com/zoonet/pictures/angoragoat.jpg

Applicable Portions: VAYIKRA – Leviticus 1:1-5:26

                        TZAV – Leviticus 6:1-8:36

                        SHEMINI – Leviticus 9:1-11:47

                        ACHARAY MOT – Leviticus 16:1-18:30

Animals: Lambs
www.mindspring.com/~zoonet/pinemoun/pictures/sheep.jpg
Applicable Portion: BO – Exodus 10:1-13:16

Animals: Living, Extinct and Endangered
www.defenders.org
www.worldwildlife.org
www.bagheera.com
Applicable Portions: BERESHEET – Genesis 1:1-6:8
    NOAH – Genesis 6:9-11:32

Animals: Locusts
www.earthlife.net/insects/images/orthopta/locusta.jpg
www.ris.net/~lawnman/bible.html
Applicable Portion: BO – Exodus 10:1-13:16

Animals: Oxen
members.aol.com/zoonet/pictures/gaur.jpg
Applicable Portions: MISHPATIM – Exodus 21:1-24:18
    KI TAYTZAY – Deuteronomy 21:10-25:19

Animals: Pigs
members.tripod.lycos.nl/piggies
Applicable Portion: SHEMINI – Leviticus 9:1-11:47

Animals: Quail
www.ngpc.state.ne.us/wildlife/quail.html
Applicable Portions: BESHALACH – Exodus 13:17-17:16
    BEHA'ALOTECHA – Numbers 8:1-12:16

Animals: Rams
raysweb.net/wildlife/pages/02.html
Applicable Portions: VAYERA – Genesis 18:1-22:24
    VAYIKRA – Leviticus 1:1-5:26
    TZAV – Leviticus 6:1-8:36

Animals: Sheep
www.mindspring.com/~zoonet/pinemoun/pictures/sheep.jpg
Applicable Portions: VAYIKRA – Leviticus 1:1-5:26
                         TZAV – Leviticus 6:1-8:36

Animals: Snakes
www.snakeworld.com
www.wnybiz.com/markheim/reptile/pic32.jpg
Applicable Portion: CHUKAT – Numbers 19:1-22:1

Archaeology: A Tel
www.tau.ac.il/~archpubs/megiddo/index.html
Applicable Portion: RE'EH – Deuteronomy 11:26-16:17

Archaeology: Ancient Coins
ancient-art.com/judbib.htm
www.hum.huji.ac.il/archaeology
Applicable Portion: KI TISA – Exodus 30:11-34:35

Archaeology: Ancient Idols
www.eliki.com/ancient/civilizations/sumerian
Applicable Portions: VAYAYTZAY – Genesis 28:10-32:3
                         VAYISHLACH – Genesis 32:4-36:43

Archaeology: Ancient Trumpets
www.christianfloral.com/stamps/instruments.htm
Applicable Portion: BEHA'ALOTECHA – Numbers 8:1-12:16

Archaeology: Bethel
www.execulink.com/~wblank/bethel.htm
Applicable Portion: VAYAYTZAY – Genesis 28:10-32:3

Archaeology: Cairo Genizah
www.lib.cam.ac.uk/Taylor-Schechter/Introduction.html
Applicable Portion: VAYISHLACH – Genesis 32:4-36:43

Archaeology: Jericho

EMuseum.mankato.msus.edu/archaeology/sites/
middle_east/jericho.html

Applicable Portions: PINCHAS – Numbers 25:10-30:1
MATOT – Numbers 30:2-32:42
MAS'AY – Numbers 33:1-36:3

Archaeology: Lamps

members.tripod.com/~Oil_Lamps

Applicable Portion: TETZAVEH – Exodus 27:20-30:10

Archaeology: Shechem

www.maxpages.com/shechem

Applicable Portion: VAYISHLACH – Genesis 32:4-36:43

Archaeology: Ur

EMuseum.mankato.msus.edu/archaeology/sites/
middle_east/ur.html

Applicable Portions: NOAH – Genesis 6:9-11:32
LECH LECHA – Genesis 12:1-17:27

Art: Marc Chagall

www.mcs.csuhayward.edu/~malek/Chagal.html

Applicable Portion: VAYAKHEL – Exodus 35:1-38:20

Art: Michelangelo's Moses

www.kfki.hu/~arthp/art/m/michelan/1sculptu/giulio_2/moses.jpg

Applicable Portion: KI TISA – Exodus 30:11-34:35

Art: Shalom of Safed

www.sternart.com/i-shalom.htm

Applicable Portion: VAYAKHEL – Exodus 35:1-38:20

Bet Alpha Synagogue in Israel – Zodiac Floor

www.hefzi.org.il/turism/betsynagogue.html

ccat.sas.upenn.edu/rs/2/Judaism/bethalpha.htm

Applicable Portion: SHOFETIM – Deuteronomy 16:18-21:9

Biographies: Modern Individuals

amillionlives.com

Applicable Portions: NOAH – Genesis 6:9-11:32

KEDOSHIM – Leviticus 19:1-20:27

Blood Libel

www.fordham.edu/halsall/source/rinn.html

Applicable Portion: RE'EH – Deuteronomy 11:26-16:17

Boats: Ancient

www.arksearch.com

www.lexiline.com/lexiline/lexi143.htm

Applicable Portion: NOAH – Genesis 6:9-11:32

Brit Milah/Circumcision

www.mishpacha.org/britabout.shtml

Applicable Portions: LECH LECHA – Genesis 12:1-17:27

VAYISHLACH – Genesis 32:4-36:43

SHEMOT – Exodus 1:1-6:1

Calendar – Jewish

www.jewfaq.org/calendar.html

kids.infoplease.lycos.com/ipka/a0777385.html

bnaibrith.org/caln.html

Applicable Portions: PIKUDAY – Exodus 38:21-40:38

EMOR – Leviticus 21:1-24:23

Challah

www.bus.ualberta.ca/yreshef/shabbat/shabcustoms.html
biblicalholidays.com/Sabbath/challah.htm
Applicable Portions: BESHALACH – Exodus 13:17-17:16
                       VAYIKRA – Leviticus 1:1-5:26
                       SHELACH LECHA – Numbers 13:1-15:41

Chevrah Kaddisha

www.shemayisrael.co.il/burial/index.htm
www.jrf.org/cjcmd/chevrapg.htm
Applicable Portion: CHAYAY SARAH – Genesis 23:1-25:18

Desert Life: Tents

www.interknowledge.com/egypt/sinai/bedouin02.htm
Applicable Portion: LECH LECHA – Genesis 12:1-17:27

Desert Life: Travel

www.interknowledge.com/egypt/sinai/bedouin.htm
Applicable Portion: VAYERA – Genesis 18:1-22:24

Desert Life: Wells

www.hia.net/kjsmith/imagint/algeria.htm
Applicable Portions: CHAYAY SARAH – Genesis 23:1-25:18
                       TOLEDOT – Genesis 25:19-28:9

Egypt: Ancient Culture

emuseum.mankato.msus.edu/prehistory/egypt/history/history.html
Applicable Portions: VAYAYSHEV – Genesis 37:1-40:23
                       MIKAYTZ – Genesis 41:1-44:17
                       VAYIGASH – Genesis 44:18-47:27
                       VAYECHI – Genesis 47:28-50:26
                       SHEMOT – Exodus 1:1-6:1
                       VAERA – Exodus 6:2-9:35
                       BO – Exodus 10:1-13:16

BESHALACH – Exodus 13:17-17:16
VAYIKRA – Leviticus 1:1-5:26
ACHARAY MOT – Leviticus 16:1-18:30

Enuma Elish (Babylonian Text)
pubpages.unh.edu/~cbsiren/assyrbabyl-faq.html
Applicable Portion: BERESHEET – Genesis 1:1-6:8

Ethical Wills
www.ethicalwill.com
Applicable Portion: VAYECHI – Genesis 47:28-50:26

Etrog
207/168.91.4/vjholidays/sukkot/minim.htm
Applicable Portion: EMOR – Leviticus 21:1-24:23

Falashas
www.geocities.com/CollegePark/7139
Applicable Portion: BALAK – Numbers 22:2-25:9

Firstborn Rights
www.newadvent.org/cathen/06081a.htm
Applicable Portions: TOLEDOT – Genesis 25:19-28:9
    BO – Exodus 10:1-13:16

First Synagogue in New York
www.eldridgestreet.org
Applicable Portion: VAYAKHEL – Exodus 35:1-38:20

Geneva Convention
www.unhchr.ch/html/menu3/b/91.htm
Applicable Portion: LECH LECHA – Genesis 12:1-17:27

Genizah

www.brittanica.com/seo/g/genizah

Applicable Portions: VAYISHLACH – Genesis 32:4-36:43

KI TISA – Exodus 30:11-34:35

RE'EH – Deuteronomy 11:26-16:17

Get (Jewish Divorce)

www.ahavat-israel.com/torat/divorce.asp

Applicable Portion: KI TAYTZAY – Deuteronomy 21:10-25:19

Gilgamesh (Babylonian Text)

pubpages.unh.edu/~cbsiren/assyrbabyl-faq.html#Gilgamesh

Applicable Portion: NOAH – Genesis 6:9-11:32

Handicapped

www.geocities.com/Athens/4611

www.usdoj.gov/crt/ada/adahom1.htm

Applicable Portions: TAZRIA – Leviticus 12:1-13:59

METZORA – Leviticus 14:1-15:33

Holidays: Chanukah

207.168.91.4/vjholidays/chanukah/index.htm

www.holidays.net/chanukah

Applicable Portion: HA'AZINU – Deuteronomy 32:1-52

Holidays: Passover

207.168.91.4/vjholidays.com/pesach/Home.htm

www.holidays.net/passover

Applicable Portions: BO – Exodus 10:1-13:16

MISHPATIM – Exodus 21:1-24:18

EMOR – Leviticus 21:1-24:23

BEHA'ALOTECHA – Numbers 8:1-12:16

PINCHAS – Numbers 25:10-30:1

DEVARIM – Deuteronomy 1:1-3:22
RE'EH – Deuteronomy 11:26-16:17
KI TAVO – Deuteronomy 26:1-29:8

Holidays: Purim

207.168.91.4/vjholidays/purim/index.htm
www.holidays.net/purim
Applicable Portion: KI TAYTZAY – Deuteronomy 21:10-25:19

Holidays: Rosh Chodesh

www.bus.ualberta.ca/yreshef/shabbat/roshframes.html
Applicable Portion: PINCHAS – Numbers 25:10-30:1

Holidays: Rosh HaShanah

207.168.91.4/vjholidays/rosh/index.htm
www.holidays.net/highholydays
Applicable Portions: EMOR – Leviticus 21:1-24:23
                        BECHUKOTAI – Leviticus 26:3-27:34
                        PINCHAS – Numbers 25:10-30:1
                        NITZAVIM – Deuteronomy 29:9-30:20

Holidays: Shabbat

www.shabat.co.il
www.jewfaq.org/shabbat.htm
www.everythingjewish.com/Shabbat/Shabbat_Origins.htm
www.ou.org/chagim/shabbat
Applicable Portions: YITRO – Exodus 18:1-20:23
                        MISHPATIM – Exodus 21:1-24:18
                        KI TISA – Exodus 30:11-34:35
                        VAYAKHEL – Exodus 35:1-38:20
                        KEDOSHIM – Leviticus 19:1-20:27
                        EMOR – Leviticus 21:1-24:23
                        BEHAR – Leviticus 25:1-26:2

NASO – Numbers 4:21-7:89
PINCHAS – Numbers 25:10-30:1
MAS'AY – Numbers 33:1-36:3
VA'ETCHANAN – Deuteronomy 3:23-7:11

Holidays: Shavuot
207.168.91.4/vjholidays/shavuot
www.holidays.net/shavuot
Applicable Portions: YITRO – Exodus 18:1-20:23
MISHPATIM – Exodus 21:1-24:18
EMOR – Leviticus 21:1-24:23
PINCHAS – Numbers 25:10-30:1
RE'EH – Deuteronomy 11:26-16:17

Holidays: Simchat Torah
207.168.91.4/vjholidays/simchatorah
Applicable Portion: V'ZOT HABRACHAH –
Deuteronomy 33:1-34:12

Holidays: Sukkot
207.168.91.4/vjholidays/sukkot
www.holidays.net/sukkot
Applicable Portions: MISHPATIM – Exodus 21:1-24:18
EMOR – Leviticus 21:1-24:23
PINCHAS – Numbers 25:10-30:1
RE'EH – Deuteronomy 11:26-16:17
VAYAYLECH – Deuteronomy 31:1-30

Holidays: Tisha B'Av
207.168.91.4/vjholidays/3weeks
Applicable Portions: SHELACH LECHA – Numbers 13:1-15:41
VA'ETCHANAN – Deuteronomy 3:23-7:11

Holidays: Yom Kippur

207.168.91.4/vjholidays/rosh/yomstep.htm

Applicable Portions: ACHARAY MOT – Leviticus 16:1-18:30

                                    EMOR – Leviticus 21:1-24:23

                                    BEHAR – Leviticus 25:1-26:2

                                    BECHUKOTAI – Leviticus 26:3-27:34

                                    PINCHAS – Numbers 25:10-30:1

                                    MATOT – Numbers 30:2-32:42

                                    NITZAVIM – Deuteronomy 29:9-30:20

Jerusalem

www.us-israel.org/jsource/vie/Jerutoc.html

Applicable Portions: VA'ETCHANAN – Deuteronomy 3:23-7:11

                                      EKEV – Deuteronomy 7:12-11:25

                                      RE'EH – Deuteronomy 11:26-16:17

Jerusalem: Church of the Holy Sepulchre

www.us-israel.org/jsource/Archaeology/church.html

Applicable Portion: VAYERA – Genesis 18:1-22:24

Jerusalem: Dome of the Rock

www.us-israel.org/jsource/Society_&_Culture/geo/
Mount.html#Dome

Applicable Portion: VAYERA – Genesis 18:1-22:24

Jerusalem: Via Dolorosa

www.us-israel.org/jsource/vie/Jerusalem2.html#Cross

Applicable Portion: VAYERA – Genesis 18:1-22:24

Jordan River

encarta.msn.com/find/Concise.asp?ti=06512000

Applicable Portions: MATOT – Numbers 30:2-32:42

                                      EKEV – Deuteronomy 7:12-11:25

Joseph's Coat

www.reallyuseful.com/joseph

Applicable Portion: VAYAYSHEV – Genesis 37:1-40:23

Judaism: Conservative

www.uscj.org

Applicable Portions: YITRO – Exodus 18:1-20:23
TETZAVEH – Exodus 27:20-30:10
TZAV – Leviticus 6:1-8:36
NASO – Numbers 4:21-7:89
KI TAYTZAY – Deuteronomy 21:10-25:19

Judaism: Orthodox

www.ou.org

Applicable Portions: YITRO – Exodus 18:1-20:23
TETZAVEH – Exodus 27:20-30:10
TZAV – Leviticus 6:1-8:36
NASO – Numbers 4:21-7:89
KI TAYTZAY – Deuteronomy 21:10-25:19

Judaism: Reconstructionist

www.jrf.org

Applicable Portions: YITRO – Exodus 18:1-20:23
TETZAVEH – Exodus 27:20-30:10
TZAV – Leviticus 6:1-8:36
NASO – Numbers 4:21-7:89
KI TAYTZAY – Deuteronomy 21:10-25:19

Judaism: Reform

www.rj.org
www.uahc.org

Applicable Portions: YITRO – Exodus 18:1-20:23
TETZAVEH – Exodus 27:20-30:10
TZAV – Leviticus 6:1-8:36

NASO – Numbers 4:21-7:89
KI TAYTZAY – Deuteronomy 21:10-25:19
NITZAVIM – Deuteronomy 29:9-30:20

Justice Symbol

www.dejohnson.com/scalesofjustice.html
Applicable Portion: SHOFETIM – Deuteronomy 16:18-21:9

Kashrut

www.kashrut.com
www.kosherfinder.com
Applicable Portions: VAYISHLACH – Genesis 32:4-36:43
MISHPATIM – Exodus 21:1-24:18
TZAV – Leviticus 6:1-8:36
SHEMINI – Leviticus 9:1-11:47
ACHARAY MOT – Leviticus 16:1-18:30
RE'EH – Deuteronomy 11:26-16:17
SHOFETIM – Deuteronomy 16:18-21:9

Ketubah

www.theketubah.com
Applicable Portions: YITRO – Exodus 18:1-20:23
VAYAKHEL – Exodus 35:1-38:20

Kiddush Cup

www.mjoe.org/ritual/kiddush1.html
www.artjudaica.com/cgi-bin/svend/gallery_kiddish
Applicable Portions: VAYAKHEL – Exodus 35:1-38:20
NASO – Numbers 4:21-7:89

Laws of Other Cultures: Code of Hammurabi

www.wsu.edu/~dee/MESO/CODE.HTM
Applicable Portions: YITRO – Exodus 18:1-20:23
MISHPATIM – Exodus 21:1-24:18

Leprosy (Hansen's Disease)
www.who.int/lep
www.cdc.gov/ncidod/dbmd/diseaseinfo/hansens_t.htm
Applicable Portions: TAZRIA – Leviticus 12:1-13:59
                         METZORA – Leviticus 14:1-15:33
                         BEHA'ALOTECHA – Numbers 8:1-12:16

Liberty Bell
www.nps.gov/inde/liberty-bell.html
Applicable Portion: BEHAR – Leviticus 25:1-26:2

Lilith
www.lilitu.com/lilith/historical.html
Applicable Portion: BERESHEET – Genesis 1:1-6:8

Lulav
207.168.91.4/vjholidays/sukkot/minim.htm
Applicable Portion: EMOR – Leviticus 21:1-24:23

Mahatma Ghandi Speeches
www.mkgandhi.org/quots.htm
Applicable Portion: DEVARIM – Deuteronomy 1:1-3:22

Maps: Ancient Egypt
www.khouse.org/blueletter/images/maps/Otest/world.jpg
Applicable Portions: VAYAYSHEV – Genesis 37:1-40:23
                         MIKAYTZ – Genesis 41:1-44:17
                         VAYIGASH – Genesis 44:18-47:27
                         VAYECHI – Genesis 47:28-50:26
                         SHEMOT – Exodus 1:1-6:1
                         VAERA – Exodus 6:2-9:35
                         BO – Exodus 10:1-13:16

Maps: Ancient Israel

www.wsu.edu/~dee/HEBREWS/ANISRMAP.HTM

Applicable Portions: LECH LECHA – Genesis 12:1-17:27

        VAYERA – Genesis 18:1-22:24

        CHAYAY SARAH – Genesis 23:1-25:18

        TOLEDOT – Genesis 25:19-28:9

        VAYAYTZAY – Genesis 28:10-32:3

        VAYISHLACH – Genesis 32:4-36:43

        VAYIGASH – Genesis 44:18-47:27

        VAYAKHEL – Exodus 35:1-38:20

        SHELACH LECHA – Numbers 13:1-15:41

        CHUKAT – Numbers 19:1-22:1

        BALAK – Numbers 22:2-25:9

        PINCHAS – Numbers 25:10-30:1

        MATOT – Numbers 30:2-32:42

        MAS'AY – Numbers 33:1-36:3

        DEVARIM – Deuteronomy 1:1-3:22

        VA'ETCHANAN – Deuteronomy 3:23-7:11

        EKEV – Deuteronomy 7:12-11:25

        SHOFETIM – Deuteronomy 16:18-21:9

        KI TAVO – Deuteronomy 26:1-29:8

        HA'AZINU – Deuteronomy 32:1-52

        V'ZOT HABRACHAH –
          Deuteronomy 33:1-34:12

Maps: Ancient Middle East

www.khouse.org/blueletter/images/maps/Otest/world.jpg

Applicable Portions: BERESHEET – Genesis 1:1-6:8

        NOAH – Genesis 6:9-11:32

        LECH LECHA – Genesis 12:1-17:27

        PIKUDAY – Exodus 38:21-40:38

Maps: Cities of Refuge

www.khouse.org/blueletter/images/maps/Otest/refuge.html

Applicable Portion: MAS'AY – Numbers 33:1-36:3

Maps: Modern Israel

www.lib.utexas.edu/Libs/PCL/Map_collection/
middle_east_and_asia/Israel.GIF

Applicable Portions: MAS'AY – Numbers 33:1-36:3

                                RE'EH – Deuteronomy 11:26-16:17

Maps: Sinai

www.khouse.org/blueletter/images/maps/Otest/sinai.gif

Applicable Portions: BESHALACH – Exodus 13:17-17:16

                                YITRO – Exodus 18:1-20:23

                                BAMIDBAR – Numbers 1:1-4:20

                                BEHA'ALOTECHA – Numbers 8:1-12:16

                                MAS'AY – Numbers 33:1-36:3

                                DEVARIM – Deuteronomy 1:1-3:22

Maps: Twelve Tribes

www.khouse.org/blueletter/images/maps/Otest/boundaries.gif

Applicable Portions: VAYECHI – Genesis 47:28-50:26

                                  MATOT – Numbers 30:2-32:42

                                MAS'AY – Numbers 33:1-36:3

Martin Luther King, Jr.: "I Have a Dream" Speech

web66.coled.umn.edu/new/MLK/MLK.html

Applicable Portion: DEVARIM – Deuteronomy 1:1-3:22

Matzah

aish.com/holidays/passover/articles/immediate_changes.asp
graphicdesign.miningco.com/arts/graphicdesign/library/
  passover/blpasclip1.htm

Applicable Portions: BO – Exodus 10:1-13:16

                                VAYIKRA – Leviticus 1:1-5:26

Megillah

207.168.91.4/vjholidays/purim/readmeg.htm

Applicable Portion: VAYAKHEL – Exodus 35:1-38:20

Menorah

www.templeinstitute.org/vessels/menorah.html

Applicable Portions: TERUMAH – Exodus 25:1-27:19

        VAYAKHEL – Exodus 35:1-38:20

        BEHA'ALOTECHA – Numbers 8:1-12:16

Mezzuzah

www.nvo.com/menshenables/mezzuzot

Applicable Portions: VA'ETCHANAN – Deuteronomy 3:23-7:11

        KI TAYTZAY – Deuteronomy 21:10-25:19

Mikvah

www.his.com/~chabad/Mikvah.htm

Applicable Portions: VAYIKRA – Leviticus 1:1-5:26

        METZORA – Leviticus 14:1-15:33

Names

www.behindthename.com

Applicable Portions: LECH LECHA – Genesis 12:1-17:27

        VAYISHLACH – Genesis 32:4-36:43

Ner Tamid

scheinerman.net/judaism/synagogue/objects2.htm#ner

Applicable Portion: TETZAVEH – Exodus 27:20-30:10

Olympic Rings

www.southcom.com.au/~jennifert/Games/rings.html

Applicable Portion: NOAH – Genesis 6:9-11:32

Organizations: AIDS Organizations

www.thebody.com/help.html

Applicable Portion: METZORA – Leviticus 14:1-15:33

Organizations: American Jewish Archives
huc.edu/aja
Applicable Portion: DEVARIM – Deuteronomy 1:1-3:22

Organizations: American Jewish Historical Society
www.ajhs.org
Applicable Portion: DEVARIM – Deuteronomy 1:1-3:22

Organizations: American Jewish World Service
www.ajws.org
Applicable Portions: MIKAYTZ – Genesis 41:1-44:17
                                 VAYIGASH – Genesis 44:18-47:27

Organizations: American Red Cross
www.redcross.org
Applicable Portion: VAYAYSHEV – Genesis 37:1-40:23

Organizations: American Red Magen David for Israel
www.armdi.org/main.html
Applicable Portion: VAYAYSHEV – Genesis 37:1-40:23

Organizations: American Society for the Protection
of Nature in Israel
just-tzedakah.org/reports/SocietyfortheProtection/basicinfo.html
www.spni.org/e/
Applicable Portion: BERESHEET – Genesis 1:1-6:8

Organizations: Amnesty International USA
www.amnesty-usa.org
Applicable Portion: MIKAYTZ – Genesis 41:1-44:17

Organizations: Bay Area Council for Jewish Rescue and Renewal
www.bacjrr.org
Applicable Portion: SHEMOT – Exodus 1:1-6:1

Organizations: Birds of Prey Foundation
www.birds-of-prey.org
Applicable Portion: KI TAYTZAY – Deuteronomy 21:10-25:19

Organizations: Coalition on the Environment and Jewish Life
www.coejl.org
Applicable Portion: CHUKAT – Numbers 19:1-22:1

Organizations: Friends of the Earth
www.foe.org
Applicable Portion: BERESHEET – Genesis 1:1-6:8

Organizations: Habitat for Humanity
www.habitat.org
Applicable Portion: PIKUDAY – Exodus 38:21-40:38

Organizations: Horse Protection League
www.hpl-colo.org
Applicable Portion: KI TAYTZAY – Deuteronomy 21:10-25:19

Organizations: Jewish Braille Institute
www.jewishbraille.org
Applicable Portion: KEDOSHIM – Leviticus 19:1-20:27

Organizations: Jewish Healing Center
www.growthhouse.org/ruachami.html
Applicable Portion: BEHA'ALOTECHA – Numbers 8:1-12:16

Organizations: Jewish National Fund
www.jnf.org
Applicable Portions: TOLEDOT – Genesis 25:19-28:9
                         BEHAR – Leviticus 25:1-26:2
                         SHOFETIM – Deuteronomy 16:18-21:9

Organizations: Jewish Vegetarian and Ecological Society

www.ivu.org/jvs

Applicable Portion: NOAH – Genesis 6:9-11:32

Organizations: Jewish Vegetarians of North America

www.orbyss.com/jvna.htm

Applicable Portion: NOAH – Genesis 6:9-11:32

Organizations: Local Tzedakah Opportunities

www.volunteermatch.org

Applicable Portions: NOAH – Genesis 6:9-11:32
VAERA – Exodus 6:2-9:35
YITRO – Exodus 18:1-20:23
KEDOSHIM – Leviticus 19:1-20:27

Organizations: MAZON

www.mazon.org

Applicable Portions: CHAYAY SARAH – Genesis 23:1-25:18
MIKAYTZ – Genesis 41:1-44:17
EKEV – Deuteronomy 7:12-11:25

Organizations: National Conference for Community and Justice (formerly the National Conference of Christians and Jews)

www.nccj.org

Applicable Portion: RE'EH – Deuteronomy 11:26-16:17

Organizations: National Congress of the Jewish Deaf (Jewish deaf links)

www.jdcc.org/links/links.html

Applicable Portion: KEDOSHIM – Leviticus 19:1-20:27

Organizations: New Israel Fund

www.nif.org/home

Applicable Portion: MATOT – Numbers 30:2-32:42

Organizations: North American Conference on Ethiopian Jewry
www.circus.org/nacoej.htm
Applicable Portions: BAMIDBAR – Numbers 1:1-4:20
  BALAK – Numbers 22:2-25:9

Organizations: Oxfam America
www.oxfamamerica.org
Applicable Portion: MIKAYTZ – Genesis 41:1-44:17

Organizations: Rabbanit Bracha Kapach
www.ziv.org/z2k_023.html
Applicable Portion: CHAYAY SARAH – Genesis 23:1-25:18

Organizations: Redistribution Center
www.ziv.org/ziv99_annprt2.html
Applicable Portion: PINCHAS – Numbers 25:10-30:1

Organizations: Sierra Club
www.sierraclub.org
Applicable Portion: BERESHEET – Genesis 1:1-6:8

Organizations: U.S. Holocaust Memorial Council
www.ushmm.org
Applicable Portion: DEVARIM – Deuteronomy 1:1-3:22

Organizations: Vegetarian Resource Group
www.vrg.org
Applicable Portion: NOAH – Genesis 6:9-11:32

Organizations: World Union for Progressive Judaism
rj.org/wupj
Applicable Portion: NITZAVIM – Deuteronomy 29:9-30:20

Organizations: World Union Task Force on Soviet Jewry (UCSJ link)
www.fsumonitor.com
Applicable Portion: SHEMOT – Exodus 1:1-6:1

Organizations: World Wildlife Fund
www.worldwildlife.org
Applicable Portion: BERESHEET – Genesis 1:1-6:8

Organizations: YIVO Institute for Jewish Research
www.yivoinstitute.org
Applicable Portion: DEVARIM – Deuteronomy 1:1-3:22

Parapet/Roof
architecture.about.com/arts/architecture/library/
blgloss-parapet.htm
Applicable Portion: KI TAYTZAY – Deuteronomy 21:10-25:19

Pidyon HaBen
www.us-israel.org/jsource/Judaism/Pidyon_Haben.html
Applicable Portions: BO – Exodus 10:1-13:16
                       KORACH – Numbers 16:1-18:32

Planets
pds.jpl.nasa.gov/planets
Applicable Portion: BERESHEET – Genesis 1:1-6:8

Pope John XXIII
www.newadvent.org/Popes/ppjo23.htm
Applicable Portion: VAYIGASH – Genesis 44:18-47:27

Rainbows
www.unidata.ucar.edu/staff/blynds/rnbw.html
australiansevereweather.simplenet.com/photography/
   photos/1994/0626mb01.jpg
Applicable Portion: NOAH – Genesis 6:9-11:32

Religions: Buddhism

www.ncf.carleton.ca/dharma/introduction/buddhism.html
buddhism.about.com/religion/buddhism/blbud101.htm
Applicable Portion: SHEMINI – Leviticus 9:1-11:47

Religions: Hinduism

www.geocities.com/RodeoDrive/1415/indexd.html
www.holyindia.org
Applicable Portion: SHEMINI – Leviticus 9:1-11:47

Religions: Islam

www.iad.org/intro/intro.html
Applicable Portion: SHEMINI – Leviticus 9:1-11:47

Sacrifices

www.www.templeinstitute.org/services/Sacrifices.html
Applicable Portion: VAYIKRA – Leviticus 1:1-5:26

Salt

www.saltinfo.com
Applicable Portion: KORACH – Numbers 16:1-18:32

Shabbat Candles

www.ucalgary.ca/~elsegal/Shokel/951102_Two_Candles.html
Applicable Portion: VAYIKRA – Leviticus 1:1-5:26

Shabbatai Zvi

www.us-israel.org/jsource/biography/Zvi.html
Applicable Portion: RE'EH – Deuteronomy 11:26-16:17

Shakespeare

tech-two.mit.edu/Shakespeare/works.html
Applicable Portion: KI TAYTZAY – Deuteronomy 21:10-25:19

Shofar

www.holidays.net/highholydays/shofar.htm
www.judaicaonline.com/CT_Misc/PRMS2_MSG427.htm
Applicable Portions: VAYERA – Genesis 18:1-22:24
                                    YITRO – Exodus 18:1-20:23
                                    EMOR – Leviticus 21:1-24:23
                                    NITZAVIM – Deuteronomy 29:9-30:20
                                    VAYAYLECH – Deuteronomy 31:1-30

Sofer (Torah Scribe)

www.thesoferstam.com/about_the_sofer.htm
www.neilyerman.com
Applicable Portion: VAYAYLECH – Deuteronomy 31:1-30

Spice Box

www.artjudaica.com/cgi-bin/svend/gallery_havdalah
www.uahc.org/ny/tinw/ReligiousLiving/ReligiousObjects/
    HavdalahRO.htm
Applicable Portion: KI TISA – Exodus 30:11-34:35

State of Israel – Symbol

www.knesset.gov.il/knesset/tour/etour2.htm
Applicable Portion: TERUMAH – Exodus 25:1-27:19

Suffrage Movement

www.pbs.org/onewoman/suffrage.html
Applicable Portion: MAS'AY – Numbers 33:1-36:3

Synagogues

www.mlandau-architects.com/synagogue.htm
Applicable Portions: TERUMAH – Exodus 25:1-27:19
                                    PIKUDAY – Exodus 38:21-40:38
                                    KEDOSHIM – Leviticus 19:1-20:27

The Tabernacle

www.domini.org/tabern/tabhome.htm

Applicable Portion: TERUMAH – Exodus 25:1-27:19

Tallit

www.mjoe.org/ritual/tallit1.html

www.artjudaica.com/cgi-bin/svend/gallery_tallit

Applicable Portions: VAYAKHEL – Exodus 35:1-38:20

PIKUDAY – Exodus 38:21-40:38

SHELACH LECHA – Numbers 13:1-15:41

Tefillin

www.tefillin.co.il

www.mjoe.org/ritual/tefillin1.html

Applicable Portions: BO – Exodus 10:1-13:16

VA'ETCHANAN – Deuteronomy 3:23-7:11

EKEV – Deuteronomy 7:12-11:25

The Ten Plagues

www.shul.org.za/pesach/plagues.html

Applicable Portions: VAERA – Exodus 6:2-9:35

BO – Exodus 10:1-13:16

Twelve Tribes

www.hadassah.org.il/chagall.htm

Applicable Portions: VAYAYTZAY – Genesis 28:10-32:3

VAYECHI – Genesis 47:28-50:26

SHEMOT – Exodus 1:1-6:1

TETZAVEH – Exodus 27:20-30:10

BAMIDBAR – Numbers 1:1-4:20

NASO – Numbers 4:21-7:89

SHELACH LECHA – Numbers 13:1-15:41

KORACH – Numbers 16:1-18:32

KI TAVO – Deuteronomy 26:1-29:8
V'ZOT HABRACHAH –
Deuteronomy 33:1-34:12

Tzitzit

www.mjoe.org/ritual/tzitzit1.html
www.exo.net/bluethread/tzitzit.htm
Applicable Portions: TETZAVEH – Exodus 27:20-30:10
KI TAYTZAY – Deuteronomy 21:10-25:19

U.S. Census Bureau

www.census.gov
Applicable Portion: BAMIDBAR – Numbers 1:1-4:20

U.S. Civil War: Slavery

www.iath.virginia.edu/utc/sitemap.html
www.jewish-history.com/civilwar.htm
Applicable Portion: RE'EH – Deuteronomy 11:26-16:17

U.S. Judicial System

encarta.msn.com/find/Concise.asp?ti=06747000
www.firstgov.gov/us_gov/judicial_branch.html
Applicable Portions: YITRO – Exodus 18:1-20:23
DEVARIM – Deuteronomy 1:1-3:22

U.S. Taxation

www.firstgov.gov/topics/money.html
Applicable Portion: KI TAVO – Deuteronomy 26:1-29:8

Vegetation: Acacia Trees

www.anbg.gov.au/acacia
Applicable Portion: VAYAKHEL – Exodus 35:1-38:20

Vegetation: Cedar Trees
www.orst.edu/instruct/for241/con/trcedgen.html
Applicable Portion: SHOFETIM – Deuteronomy 16:18-21:9

Vegetation: Cedar Wood
www.orst.edu/instruct/for241/con/trcedgen.html
Applicable Portion: METZORA – Leviticus 14:1-15:33

Vegetation: Cypress Trees
www.orst.edu/instruct/for241/con/cyprgen.html
Applicable Portion: SHOFETIM – Deuteronomy 16:18-21:9

Vegetation: Fig Trees
aggie-horticulture.tamu.edu/extension/homefruit/fig/fig.html
Applicable Portion: PINCHAS – Numbers 25:10-30:1

Vegetation: Fruit Bearing Trees
www.virtualorchard.net
Applicable Portion: SHOFETIM – Deuteronomy 16:18-21:9

Vegetation: General
endeavor.des.ucdavis.edu/cnps/thums.asp
Applicable Portion: BERESHEET – Genesis 1:1-6:8

Vegetation: Grapes
osu.orst.edu/food-resource/images/FRUITVEG/GRAPES/
    on_vine(ac).jpg
wine.about.com/food/wine/library/encyc/bl_grapes_primer/.htm
Applicable Portions: SHELACH LECHA – Numbers 13:1-15:41
                         HA'AZINU – Deuteronomy 32:1-52

Vegetation: Hyssop (Moss)
www.chatlink.com/~herbseed/hyssop.htm
Applicable Portion: METZORA – Leviticus 14:1-15:33

Vegetation: Non–fruit Bearing Trees

www.orst.edu/instruct/for241/con/trcedgen.html

Applicable Portion: SHOFETIM – Deuteronomy 16:18-21:9

Vegetation: Olive Trees

www.gilboa.co.il/ol-tree.htm

Applicable Portion: NOAH – Genesis 6:9-11:32

                        TETZAVEH – Exodus 27:20-30:10

                        EMOR – Leviticus 21:1-24:23

                        HA'AZINU – Deuteronomy 32:1-52

Vegetation: Pomegranates

www.pomegranateconnection.com/history.htm

www.tcsn.net/chadmark/pomegranate.htm

Applicable Portion: TETZAVEH – Exodus 27:20-30:10

Vegetation: Tamarisk Trees

www.members.tripod.com/~bbowles/tamarisk.html

Applicable Portion: CHAYAY SARAH – Genesis 23:1-25:18

Vegetation: Wheat

www.crop.cri.nz/foodinfo/millbake/whgrain.htm

Applicable Portion: HA'AZINU – Deuteronomy 32:1-52

Weddings

www.ohr.org.il/judaism/articles/wedding.htm

Applicable Portions: CHAYAY SARAH – Genesis 23:1-25:18

                        VAYAYTZAY – Genesis 28:10-32:3

                        SHOFETIM – Deuteronomy 16:18-21:9

Wrongdoing by Public Officials

www.villagevice.com

Applicable Portion: VAYIKRA – Leviticus 1:1-5:26

Yahrzeit
www.yahrzeit.org/yizkor.html
Applicable Portion: V'ZOT HABRACHAH –
                       Deuteronomy 33:1-34:12

Yitzhak Rabin Speeches
www.ariga.com/peacebiz/rabin/lastrabn.htm
Applicable Portion: DEVARIM – Deuteronomy 1:1-3:22

Zionists: Early Chalutzim
www.jajz-ed.org.il/100/time/index.html
Applicable Portion: DEVARIM – Deuteronomy 1:1-3:22

Part III:
Commentator Resources

This section provides background material on various Torah commentators mentioned in *Teaching Torah*. Information on the lives and work of many of the most significant scholars can be found through these URLs. Be aware that the majority of material comes in the form of a reference in someone else's commentary, rather than as specific biographical information. Generally, this section does not include contemporary commentators, whose work is current and readily available commercially. If a particular writer is not listed here, refer to "What to Do If Something Can't Be Found Online" (page xix) for tips on how to search for online resources quickly.

Abravanel, Isaac
www.jtsa.edu/users/hsp/htm/empowere.html

Bar Kappara
www.aishdas.org/webshas/torah/amora/bkappara.htm

Ben Zakkai, Yohanan
www.us-israel.org/jsource/biography/ben_zakkai.html

Buber, Martin
www.us-israel.org/jsource/biography/Buber.html

Caro, Joseph
www.us-israel.org/jsource/biography/Caro.html

Gamaliel II, Rabban
ivanlewis.com/History/Gamaliel.html

Ginzberg, Louis
www.jewishculture.org/scholarship/99schorsch.htm

Hertz, Joseph Herman
www.chiefrabbi.org/history/hertz.html

Heschel, Abraham Joshua
www.crosscurrents.org/heschel.htm

Hillel I, The Elder
www.us-israel.org/jsource/biography/hillel.html

Hirsch, Samson Raphael
www.us-israel.org/jsource/biography/Hirsch.html

Ibn Ezra, Abraham
www.us-israel.org/jsource/biography/IbnEzra.html

Josephus, Flavius
www.us-israel.org/jsource/biography/Josephus.html

Kook, Abraham Isaac
www.us-israel.org/jsource/biography/Rav_Kook.html

Leibowitz, Nehama
www.ou.org/yerushalayim/lezikaronolam/nehama/
rememberingnehama.html

Malbim (Meir Leibush ben Yehiel Michel)
www.biu.ac.il/JH/Eparasha/vayikra/geller.html

Moses ben Jacob of Coucy
www.jewishgates.org/personalities/semag.stm

Radak (David Kimchi)
members.aol.com/LazerA/radak.html

Rambam (Maimonides – Moses ben Maimon)
www.us-israel.org/jsource/biography/Maimonides.html

Ramban (Nachmanides – Moses ben Nachman)
www.us-israel.org/jsource/biography/Nachmanides.html

Rashbam (Samuel ben Meir)
www.us-israel.org/jsource/biography/Rashbam.html

Rashi (Shlomo ben Yitzhak)
www.us-israel.org/jsource/biography/rashi.html

Sforno (Obadiah ben Jacob)
www.ucalgary.ca/~elsegal/TalmudMap/MG/MGSforno.html

Vilna Gaon (Elijah ben Solomon Zalman)
www.us-israel.org/jsource/biography/vilnagaon.html

Conclusion

This book has provided you with countless Internet resources related to *Parashat HaShavua*. Just imagine the potential for your class! A discussion of the journeys of Abraham or Moses and the Israelites will be so much more exciting and engaging using maps of the ancient Middle East. When a student wonders what an olive tree looks like, you can immediately produce a picture of one. If you decide to write to a service organization about a Tzedakah project based in some way on a particular portion, you can contact that organization and probably receive an e-mail response within a day or two.

This is not a fantasy, nor is it Jewish science fiction. This is the reality available to you now, thanks to the limitless resources of what we can call "The Ultimate Jewish Teacher Resource Center" — the Internet. In just minutes you and your curriculum can be "wired into Teaching Torah." Enjoy the journey!

APPENDIX A
Glossary of Terms

address
The location of a site on the Internet, usually beginning with "http://www." or just www. (sometimes they begin with numbers); also referred to as the URL of the site

bookmark
A favorite site that you place in a special menu on your browser, thereby enabling you to link instantaneously to that site simply by clicking on the name. In Netscape Navigator these are called "Bookmarks"; in Microsoft Internet Explorer, they are called "Favorites."

browser
The software that allows you to view sites on the Internet

cyberspace/ cyberworld
The world of the Internet and online services

directory
A site that lists other Internet sites by category, similar in function to a search engine

e-mail
Mail messages sent electronically from one computer to another; an e-mail address contains the person's user name, the "@" sign, and then the domain name

font   The style and size of type for the text on your computer screen and on your printout

GIF   One type of graphic file that is used on Internet sites

graphic   The term for drawings, pictures, or artistic word designs that are used on the Internet

home page   An Internet site dedicated to a topic or a personal interest; home pages are the format that individuals and businesses use to promote their interests on the Internet

Internet   The overall term used to describe the global system of networked computers which allow the transfer of information and communication between users; in this book, it also refers to all online services: the World Wide Web, telnet, news groups, and e-mail services and systems

JPG or JPEG   Another type of graphic file used on Internet sites, usually for photographs

key word   A primary word used for a subject search at a web site; also referred to as "search term." (To users of America Online, a "key word" takes you to a specific content area of the AOL site.)

link   Words, phrases, or graphics that when "clicked on," or "selected," provide a direct connection to another Internet site

meta-search   Conducting a search for content on the Internet using a search engine that searches other search engines and displays a range of results

online   Being connected to the Internet through a per-
                           sonal computer

root page   The foundation page of a particular web site, to
                           which all other pages of that site are linked.
                           Generally, this is the first part of the URL, ending
                           in ".com," ".org," ".gov," etc.

search engine   A "directory assistance" for the Internet which
                           allows a user to locate sites whose titles or
                           descriptions contain specific search words

site   Another name for a home page location on the
                           Internet

URL   Short for "Universal Resource Locator"; also
                           known as an address; the official location of a
                           site on the Internet

web site/   Another name for a home page — the information
web page   someone or some company places at a particular
                           URL

World Wide Web   For all practical purposes, another name for the
                           Internet

APPENDIX B
How to "Bookmark" a Web Site

Your web browser software allows you to save the address of a specific web page so that you can revisit it quickly and easily, without having to type in the complete address each time. In Microsoft Internet Explorer, these saved pages are called "Favorites;" in Netscape Navigator or Communicator, they are known as "Bookmarks." When you come across a site that you find valuable and may wish to view again, follow the instructions below for adding that site to your list of Favorites or Bookmarks.

In Microsoft Internet Explorer:
1. While online, go to the page you want to add to your Favorites list.
2. On the **Favorites** menu, click **Add to Favorites**.
3. You can accept the name of the site as shown, or type a new name for the page if you wish, something that will make sense to you in the future.

To open one of your favorite pages, click the **Favorites** menu, and from the drop-down menu, click the page you wish to open.

In Netscape Navigator or Communicator:
4. While online, go to the web page you want to bookmark.
5. Click **Bookmarks** (on a Macintosh, open the Bookmarks menu by clicking on the green bookmark icon to the right of the Go menu).
6. Choose **Add Bookmark**.

To revisit a bookmarked web page, click **Bookmarks** on the toolbar and choose a bookmarked page from the dropdown menu. (On a Macintosh, open the **Bookmarks** menu by clicking on the green bookmark icon.)